A SELF-DEVELOPMENT PROGRAMME
Constructive appraisals

Acknowledgements:
I would like to acknowledge the help from my clients
and friends who provided invaluable input and support
during the writing of this book, and Ed, who kept the
IT side running.

A SELF-DEVELOPMENT PROGRAMME

Constructive appraisals

THE ESSENTIAL GUIDE TO THINKING AND WORKING SMARTER

Roy Lecky-Thompson

MARSHALL PUBLISHING • LONDON

To Pat and my long-suffering family for their unfailing
support and constructive appraisal of my efforts.

A Marshall Edition
Conceived, edited and
designed by
Marshall Editions Ltd
The Orangery
161 New Bond Street
London W1Y 9PA

First published in the UK
in 1999 by
Marshall Publishing Ltd

Copyright © 1999
Marshall Editions
Developments Ltd

ISBN 1-84028-200-2

Cover photography
Tony Stone Images

Series Consultant Editor
Chris Roebuck
Project Editor
Conor Kilgallon
Design
Joanna Stawarz
Art Director
Sean Keogh
Managing Art Editor
Patrick Carpenter
Managing Editor
Clare Currie
Editorial Assistant
Dan Green
Editorial Coordinator
Becca Clunes
Production
Nikki Ingram
Cover Design
Poppy Jenkins

Originated in Italy by
Articolor
Printed and bound in
Portugal by Printer
Portuguesa

Video Arts quotes extracted from training films:

pp 9, 17, 57: "The Dreaded Appraisal"
pp 36, 51: "How Am I Doing?"

Contents

1

What is appraisal?
Changes in appraisals
Achieving excellence

Appraisal and business strategy

Developing the individual

Case studies

What is appraisal?

"Once I'd got appraisal up and running in my company, there was no doubt that it helped transform the way we do things, and made us much more productive. As a process, it is now central to our human resources policy." **Managing Director**

Staff appraisal goes by many different names. Some common terms are staff assessment, employee review, staff reporting, performance review and performance evaluation, or it is described in one of a number of other ways that are suitable for particular organizations. With slightly different emphases, the intentions are usually similar. Unlikely to be found in companies that employ less than 20 people, but common in organizations above 500, the appraisal process – which is what we will call it – is an integral part of human resource management throughout the public and private sector. When successful, it can not only provide

CASE STUDY

Having established his company five years ago in the rapidly developing IT support industry, Jim had a flexible and reactive approach to business opportunities, which had worked well so far. As a Managing Director with 125 staff members, it was now time, he felt, to set up an appraisal system, partly because he could not be sure he knew any more what all his staff were like, and partly because in his team of senior managers there were two he did not rate highly even though they had been with the company for a couple of years. It was probably time that they were told what he thought of them and Jim thought that writing things down would surely help. He could then freeze their salaries for a while and they would probably improve pretty sharply. They were not so bad that that they should be dismissed; in fact their technical expertise was probably sound and essential for the next couple of years.

Jim saw no reason to spend money on some external help to start up the appraisal process. He recalled how it had been done when he was a senior manager in another company ten years ago, and dug up his papers and forms from his files at home. Using technology to the full he scanned in the paper work at home, amended a few minor points, and instructed his PA on Monday to put the item as an extra item on the Executive Committee's meeting that day. When the meeting ran out of time, it didn't really matter since the papers were self explanatory. He told the executive committee that appraisal had to be done within the next month.

Jim spent a couple of evenings completing the forms on the two senior managers whom he would appraise himself. He felt he should be direct in his comments. He met each of them for fifteen minutes the following week, and gave them the completed forms. He felt certain this would help improve things. He could not understand their hostile reaction. Within two months, both of the managers had joined competitors at a significant cost to the business. What did Jim do wrong?

data for salary reviews, training, performance improvement, and career development, it can also be a useful way of helping management and staff to clarify goals that will benefit both. It can be the key foundation in effective human resource management.

Appraisal therefore is a formal means, usually once a year, of reviewing each staff member's performance, considering future aims and addressing any training or development needs.

Effectiveness

Its effectiveness depends on a number of factors. When run well, staff appraisal helps employers and employees alike, providing an ideal opportunity to "stimulate a renewed commitment from employees by telling them that their role is valued by the organization" (Video Arts, *The Dreaded Appraisal*) – in other words, making them feel appreciated. Often the result is improved productivity.

However, when appraisal does not work well, it becomes a burden on the organization and an intense source of dissatisfaction to members of staff. Unfortunately, the experience of many businesses is needlessly negative. Appraisal can be seen as embarrassing and confrontational.

There are no simple answers; but by putting a number of preconditions in place, a successful and effective appraisal process will usually result. By the end of this book, you, as a middle or senior manager, or perhaps head of your own company, will appreciate the value to your organization of an effective appraisal system. You will also know how to implement the process, evaluate its results and avoid the pitfalls. Like any new venture, the chances of failure, without the requisite planning, are high.

"In appraisal, the accent is on praise"

Questions for managers

If you are a manager contemplating an appraisal process for the first time or wanting to do something about improving current practice, it could be worth asking yourself some essential questions:

■ Why do I want to appraise staff in the first place?

■ What are my business priorities and plan for the next year; how will appraisal help?

■ What are my management colleagues saying about the subject of appraisal?

■ What do staff say and feel?

■ How do my management – and I – regard the people practices in the organization?

■ Have my managers and I been trained in non-technical skills, such as basic supervision?

■ What kind of day-to-day feedback and guidance do I and other managers give their staff?

■ Do we use the word "support" in our conversations about staff?

■ How much time, effort and resources will my organization put into setting up or amending the appraisal process?

■ How will I know when it is working properly?

Changes in appraisal in the last 10 years

The concept of appraising staff is not new. The armed forces, for example, have long had confidential reports on staff that are used to determine their future, and the public service still uses the term "reporting officer" for the appraiser and "box marking" for the rating or grading given to an employee.

The original approach to appraisal was that it was confidential in the sense that the individual might not even get to know the full contents of the report. In some organizations, the employee might see a summary; in others, the supervisor might tell the member of staff what was being said to the next level in the hierarchy. Where appraisals tried to consider the potential of an individual (usually in the form of a future job grade), this was never shown to an individual.

Development of appraisals

Over time, businesses began to feel that the appraiser's written commentary could be set against specific tasks performed by an individual in the past year; that this required the employee's active input; and that the written report could then be discussed with the individual. He or she would then write down comments after the meeting in a small space provided on the form before it was sent up the hierarchy to the boss's

boss. The performance ratings would affect the employee's pay rise, depending on the job grade. It was not entirely clear what happened to the completed form once the "grandfather" (the appraiser's boss) had signed it off, but the form could be dusted off the following year if needed. The concept of judging potential was quietly dropped. This process still exists in many organizations.

Appraisals today

By contrast, in the last few years, forward-thinking organizations have begun to see self-appraisal as a useful means to improve their human resource (HR) management practices. The full appraisal forms are completed after the self-assessment process has taken place, and more importantly, after the interview, rather than beforehand. Both parties make preparations beforehand to try to achieve a useful outcome and spend time looking at potential for individual training and development. Performance ratings may still exist in these organizations, but provide only one input into salary and bonus calculations.

Other organizations go further and now consider the detailed competencies that are required to help identify what is required in a particular post; or extend the appraisal process to obtain input from subordinates and peers.

Many appraisal processes are incomplete and do not fulfil their potential because the ultimate aims are not clear or because users are not adept at day-to-day people management. They sometimes see appraisal as a substitute.

In the rest of this chapter, we will consider the links to everyday operational management and each of the possible objectives of an appraisal system. You can then establish your priorities.

Appraisal and daily management of staff

As a manager, you have been appointed to your position because of your technical expertise. Engineer, marketer, lawyer, or financier, you have been promoted over the years because you are better than your peers, have a certain flair, and are reasonably skilled at office politics.

On your way up, you may have been trained in people management skills, but if so, you are probably the exception. Your colleagues may well have missed out, and if you talk with them about the core skills of management, they are confused by concepts such as objective setting, delegation, motivation, coaching, development, handling grievances, reviewing and rewarding performance, handling marginal outputs and so on. They may say they do these things anyway, or that it is something "the

personnel people do". Or, they argue, "we can do it at appraisal time, when you get it going".

In many cases, if you were to ask their subordinates (or get a third party to do so and carry out an audit), you might well find that staff mention their respect for their manager's technical skill – but maybe not much else.

Feedback

It is therefore an essential prerequisite for any appraisal process that reasonable attempts are made at constructive feedback on performance, agreement of goals, and coaching to help improvement in a way that encourages the outputs from staff. Your staff need to be treated as assets rather than liabilities, otherwise implementing or upgrading appraisal in isolation will not work.

So what are the specific practical uses for appraisal as an integral part of effective management?

Rewards for good performers

Most organizations aim to reward their staff in a way that reflects their value to the senior management. This may be called merit or performance-related pay. The better staff – however that is defined – are paid relatively more than their peers, either in the form of higher adjustments each year to their basic salaries, or, increasingly, by way of one-off bonuses.

Usually, this superior performance is shown through higher outputs and greater achievements, and even with teamwork, the higher relative pay of key individuals is seen to be critical. Even in incremental pay systems, there are attempts to differentiate between levels of performance.

Obtaining information

How do you obtain information on performance as an organization grows? How can you quantify statements from managers that some individuals are actually better than others and no favouritism is present? Effective appraisal can help. In many organizations, there are clear illustrative statements to differentiate better performance from the norm. This clarity helps when there is a rating scale of, say, one to five against which staff are assessed. So long as there are agreed performance objectives against which performance can be properly assessed, senior managers may begin to recognize better performance.

In some businesses, the performance rating may automatically translate into an increment: thus a rating of one may generate twice the amount of money as a rating of three. In others, the ratings or general statements are used in evidence at the time of the annual awards.

Underperformance

Evidence about underperformance can also be gleaned from appraisal. Usually couched in excessively careful terms by managers not wishing to offend marginal staff, appraisal comments can provide the data that is needed to justify below average pay adjustments or zero bonuses where specific agreed targets have not been met. Ideally, these form the basis for improvements in performance as part of an employee's continuous development. Most employers have c.10 to 20 percent of their staff not fully performing at any one time and you need to have some low pay adjustments to balance the higher ones. A below the norm rating results in a lower or nil adjustment.

LEGAL IMPLICATIONS

At a time of increasing employment litigation, employers need to have clear evidence of poor performance in case an employee is fired and claims unfair dismissal. Many an employment tribunal case has been upheld when an employee, dismissed for alleged poor performance or poor attitude over the years, demonstrates that three months before being dismissed, the appraisal was satisfactory and that there had been a subsequent pay rise. Conversely, a marginal performance appraisal can often indicate a deteriorating output, and could provide good prior evidence for dismissal if performance does not improve.

Likewise, discrimination claimants on race or gender grounds may often use evidence from appraisals to show that, for example, promotion was promised and not delivered, and completed appraisal forms are sometimes mis-used in redundancy selection criteria.

Evidence such as appraisals – or the lack of proper ones – can normally be found in employment litigation, and current trends point to even greater care being needed in recording and disclosing information.

Delivery of business strategy: key objectives

If the legal advantages of getting appraisals up and running and doing them well seem a touch defensive, then a more positive use of appraisals in day-to-day management is to help you deliver your organization's goals through your people.

Typically, as the business has grown and faced economic and competitive challenges, you and your colleagues have gradually developed a strategy that was originally designed to keep financiers happy. This strategy should now be evolving to provide a structure for action in the next couple of years, that may now be summarized and communicated throughout your company so that staff have a reasonable understanding of what the senior team are trying to do.

Each department or business unit has a strategy for the next couple of years as well. The first year often translates into budgetary and financial targets. But who is actually going to make it all happen? In practice, while the senior team remains accountable, the actual responsibility lies with the heads of units and their staff.

Knowing what to do

And do they actually know what they are supposed to do and how they will do it? They are not clairvoyants, and while you want to encourage them in their free thinking, you may have had recent experience where colleagues wrongly assumed a level of knowledge among each other about goals both individual and organizational.

Thus, agreeing specific future objectives and standards of performance with each member of staff once a year forms an essential foundation for effective appraisal, allowing logical assessment a year later. It also provides the main way of implementing a business strategy at the operating level so that all employees are pulling in the same corporate direction, which applies to all staff, even at the most junior level.

CASE STUDY 1

A professional services firm in the North West had grown rapidly to reach a total of 300 staff. A review of exit interviews of leavers showed one common factor – a lack of communication at below senior management level about the overall direction of the organization.

The firm instituted a policy of an annual staff meeting, coupled with monthly briefings. With the overall direction clear, departmental managers and team leaders were given the responsibility of translating the strategy into departmental, team and individual goals. These were reinforced through the appraisal process. Improvements took two years to implement, and resulted in lower avoidable staff wastage and greater productivity.

CASE STUDY 2

The board of a medium-sized specialist instruments company had aspirations to double its revenue over a period of five years in a fiercely competitive market. Larger competitors were heavily discounting products for customers and were poaching the company's sales professionals. In the first six months of the plan, performance was 40 percent below budget.

The sales manager recognized that she needed to translate the board's strategic aspirations into concrete objectives based on the reality of the market. She persuaded the MD that a pragmatic, revised business plan could be drawn up after an analysis of the company's strengths, weaknesses, opportunities and threats. This review included input she obtained from the sales team on the challenges of the market and what the team could actually deliver.

When the revised goals emerged, they were translated into key individual and team targets. These were to form the basis of a new performance planning and review mechanism, coupled with continuous training to support individual personal development. Within a year, the company was on target.

Achieving excellence and continuous improvement

If you look at the management books in an airport departure lounge, you will see that the word "quality" is used throughout. Successful companies need to be quality driven, and obsessed with the concept of continuous improvement – *kaizen*, as the Japanese say – to achieve world-class status.

Getting it right first time, zero defects, embracing the customer and so on are all valid aims. The challenge arises when you and your colleagues want to translate these goals into action at the operating level. You may exhort your staff and tell them what is expected; you may even involve them in the process of agreeing priorities, but unless you listen actively to the issues the staff reporting to you raise, help motivate and inspire them and engender commitment to the organization, then your business will underperform.

Motivation and quality

Of course you are not just going to do this at appraisal time, but appraisal can be positively used as a motivator and can be used to reinforce high-level corporate initiatives at the operating level. We will see later how appraisals can inspire staff.

If, on the other hand, appraisals are done in isolation from corporate initiatives, an opportunity is lost and the business runs the risk of inconsistency. Some companies feel strongly that they should compare themselves to a number of other organizations to ensure that they move from just good, to best, practice. Others want to go further, and achieve externally verifiable quality standards such as Investors in People or the European Quality Award.

In all cases, the testing for the standards reached involves checking exactly how consistent the organization is in its behaviour and how staff are helped in their continuous improvement.

Effective appraisals and their follow-up actions become key to progress on two levels – both in the organization as a whole and within individual departments or divisions.

Training and development of the individual – the organization's needs

The business world of today now focuses on rapidly changing, flexible workforces competing in the global economy. For example, obligatory modern IT skills were unheard of a generation ago and will be replaced tomorrow by requirements yet to be identified. Continuous change in an uncertain world is all taken as normal, and investment in the human capital of your organization is essential.

Developing a competitive edge in partnership with your staff is a practical goal for forward-thinking businesses. The recent joint Department for Trade and Industry/Department for Education and Employment (DTI/DfEE) report on how innovative companies brought the best out of their people to achieve significantly enhanced business performance stated that successful organizations regard their staff as their most valuable resource, which needs to be developed on an on-going basis. If a company is to realize its full potential, it has to assess the existing skills of all its employees in order to decide what extra learning and training will be needed. Then as the workforce becomes more skilled, the company can become more ambitious because the full ability of its staff is released.

The role of appraisal

Where does appraisal fit into all this? Since appraisal will often be the one time in a year when manager and subordinate have over an hour together to talk about both performance and development (to augment day-to-day feedback), it becomes a very useful way of identifying training and development needs to help deliver improved performance. Managers and subordinates identify the gaps between current and desirable performance, and agree actions. These may be in the form of internal or external courses, coaching on the job, structured reading, a brief secondment and so on.

They will also ideally consider development issues. Firstly, what steps employees might want to take to broaden their job and secondly, what they might want to do next as the organizational needs develop.

If your company has a good training policy in place, an effective appraisal process provides one of the best vehicles to encourage appropriate training for individual development.

"Try listening, you might learn something"

AS THE DTI/DfEE SAYS:

"Companies report that training and learning steadily develop an atmosphere of problem solving and creativity. Whilst at first the emphasis may be on enhanced job competency, very soon the employees will enjoy and request further learning opportunities to develop themselves more fully. These companies are fully aware of the dire consequence of neglecting their employees because experience shows that an unable, unwilling, unresponsive and unskilled workforce can undermine and negate even the best strategies.

On the other hand, companies which are managing the development of their people show enhanced performance because their employees are able, consistent, cooperative, responsible and solvers of problems. Structured approaches to people development such as Investors in People have been shown to be of particular benefit."

Development of the individual

There is a new and emerging dimension on training and development that takes thinking further. Whereas 10 years ago training and development needs were driven almost entirely by what an employer might need, there is now a distinct shift of emphasis to recognize the personal development needs of individuals as well.

Maintaining employability

The approach to employment is rapidly changing and the emphasis on careers for life has been reduced. Most staff are now conscious of the need to maintain their employability. They see the need to negotiate an acceptable "psychological contract" with you as their employer. While they hope that their future career will be looked after by you, they recognize the absence of guarantees in today's working world and that changing financial circumstances or mergers can result in enforced redundancies. They do not want to face redundancy with no chance of moving on to a new challenge through lack of skills.

To achieve this, at recruitment and at appraisal, they will want to ask how they can maintain and enhance their own knowledge and skills, and consider what investment you are prepared to put into them. These are the kind of questions that most current managers and directors would not have dared put to their bosses 20 years ago. If you have your Training and Development Policy in place, then it is possible to anticipate these needs and plan for the discussion.

Taking stock

Some companies find that it is possible to share the costs of training initiated by individuals; others are prepared to provide individual learning accounts so staff know what can be spent on a long-term investment such as an MBA.

Either way, appraisal time provides a good opportunity for a stock-take.

Younger professional staff may go further. They expect to make demands of their managers and want to know how they will be supervised, what support they will receive, and even what training you – as their boss – have had in management and coaching techniques. Since the most effective professionals will usually have a choice of employer, your response can be critical to their recruitment and retention.

Two-way process

Your staff's demands of you may be especially clear at appraisal time. For many employees, appraisal is a two-way process that includes upward feedback. Your staff will be quite clear year after year what their expectations are of you and the organization.

Partnership with staff means mutual respect and active listening to their needs. Appraisal becomes one means to achieve that end within an overall human resource policy. It is a far cry from the one way reports on staff a generation ago.

So what are your priorities in looking at appraisal? How do you get started?

If I was a typical individual employee in a company, what training would I want? I would ask for:

- Commitment to continuous training beyond the induction course I completed last year
- Access to the appropriate training each year to help improve my knowledge and skills
- Good feedback on my progress from my boss to help decide on the most appropriate training each year
- Attention to some of my ideas about my job and any appropriate courses
- Some information on the training budget and how it is worked out
- Some ideas on how I might progress in the company, and clarity on who is responsible for my career development. (I think it should be me, but with my boss's help.)
- A boss who really supports and encourages me, and won't stand in my way if I want to move to another department in a couple of years if there's a good opportunity there
- Encouragement if I want to take a qualification at night-class, perhaps through some time off for revision
- Proper records for my file that show what and how I've been doing if my boss leaves.

2

**Self-assessment
Does appraisal make
a difference?
Processes and systems**

Who does the appraisal?

Common problems

Questionnaire

Where are you now?

In this chapter, we will firstly explore some of the typical problems that arise in businesses where appraisal is going wrong, and then consider the issues for those organizations considering appraisal for the first time. The newcomer to the appraisal process might want to consider the typical problems so that they can be minimized in the future.

To help you assess where you are in your thinking and what you might need to do, check the following:

IF YOU CURRENTLY HAVE AN APPRAISAL PROCESS THAT GIVES YOU CONCERN:

■ What do you feel is going wrong?
■ What do you and your colleagues know could be improved?
■ What have your managers and staff said about appraisal?
■ Are its original aims still valid? Has your organization changed since appraisal was introduced?
■ Are your priorities (see chapter one) clear?
■ Are business aims clear?
■ Is it the system that is not right; or is it the actual application of appraisal?
■ What are your overall personnel policies and practices like?

IF YOU ARE THINKING OF INTRODUCING APPRAISAL:

■ What are your priorities for appraisal (see chapter one)?
■ How clear are your business aims and priorities?
■ What are your operational priorities in the next six months?
■ How effective are your personnel policies generally?
■ How effective is your top team in people management?
■ What do staff generally feel about working in your enterprise?
■ What are they going to say about appraisal?
■ How have you tested their expectations and reactions?

"My manager told me one day that we were going to have appraisal for the first time and said there were some forms from Personnel. His boss, whom I've hardly met, then wrote a report saying I had underperformed. When I complained, he rewrote it. The whole thing was disastrous and apparently the company is going to try again with something different this year. It must be Personnel that's to blame."
Area customer relations assistant, Fast-Moving Consumer Goods company (FMCG)

The current appraisal process: How do you measure efficiency and effectiveness in what you have now?

You may well feel that although you have had appraisal in place for some time, and that the forms are generally completed, it does not seem to make much difference and managers are not really interested.

However, since you are probably not an expert, there is no substitute for getting some evidence to check both efficiency (the process is done on time) and effectiveness (it makes a difference). This evidence can come either formally through independently run focus groups or attitude surveys or informally through simply talking to managers and staff (walking the job).

Things to remember about current appraisal procedures:

- Most staff most of the time will complain about a policy and practice if the results are not in line with their expectations or if they are not sold on the idea
- Their expectations may not always be realistic
- They may have had justifiably poor appraisals but fail to understand the real reasons why
- They may have seen poorly performing colleagues "get away with it"
- They may have been the victims of poor managers
- Managers may not see appraisal as an operational priority that affects financial outcomes
- In the knowledge sector, professionals are skilled in finding the one percent that is wrong rather than the 99 percent that is right about policy and practice, and then dismissing the whole concept
- It is a rare organization that can truthfully say its staff welcome appraisal (although you want to help yours become one).

Common problems 1

"My interview lasted ten minutes having been put off twice; and the boss just produced last year's form to regurgitate. It was pathetic." Manager, financial services company.

To help your diagnosis, in the next few pages we will explore some of the common problems that occur in appraisal systems that are both inefficient and ineffective. This is not a substitute for proper analysis in your business, but it might help your thinking and encourage you to probe. These are the key issues:

■ Who "owns" the process; is it seen as a Personnel initiative? Are the forms irrelevant? Are interviews postponed?
■ Managers are not clear who is supposed to do it or do not bother
■ There is inadequate preparation
■ There is inadequate application or follow up
■ Medium-term follow-up actions (on training for example) do not happen
■ It does not seem to improve individuals or the business.

Ownership and relevance of the process

Where appraisal has been in place some time – perhaps five years – it may well be seen as an annual exercise that emerges from Personnel a few months before salary review time. Forms are dispatched with instructional notes; last year's completed forms are dusted off from file on request; and line managers are told that they have a limited time to complete the exercise. Some may be used to the routine and see it as no more than that; others, having recently joined the company may be doing appraisal for the first time and trying to make it work.

The Personnel Manager or the Company Secretary chases the forms, hopes to achieve an 80 percent plus return rate and is satisfied when this happens – usually well after the deadline to accommodate postponed interviews. The exercise may then be considered successful. There is no check on quality of the process or the outcomes. Getting appraisal out of the way is enough.

In a recent audit of appraisal in a medium-size company, I established that the single most annoying issue that degraded the process in the eyes of staff was last-minute postponement of interviews. This happened in 40 percent of cases. A postponement by even one day was taken as a signal that managers simply did not care and that their staff were irrelevant.

"I was really pleased when I achieved a 75 percent return rate for the forms, and had my assistant file them within a week.
It was a job done for another year."
Personnel Manager

Other flaws

This may not be the only flaw in the process – in the five years since appraisal was launched, the organization may have changed; new departments created where appraisal forms (or questions on them) are less relevant, managers who were sponsors of the original aims have left, and newcomers not trained. Moreover, a new generation of younger staff has arrived who are expecting appraisal to be a more positive process than it actually is.

You may well feel that the whole exercise somehow operates in isolation from you and your colleagues' business priorities and staff needs. It probably does. There may be a smooth mechanical process in place. But is it a total waste of time? If you missed appraisal out for one year, would there be sighs of relief?

There are companies which go through the appraisal ritual each year, with enthusiasm from some departments but lack of support from others where the management style of a head of department is not appraisal-friendly. The more important that maverick department is in generating revenue, the less likely it is that appraisal will be effective elsewhere in the organization. An excellent review process in the accounts department does not help if the sales department ignores it.

Who does the appraisal?

It may seem obvious that appraisal should be carried out by an appraisee's immediate boss as the individual who knows most about the employee's job. In a number of organizations that may not be the case. For example, in some larger companies with a strict hierarchy, only those people with the job title of Manager are allowed to carry out appraisals. These people may be three grade levels above the individual being appraised and may only come across the individual in passing during the year. The most diligent may consult about the individual's performance and contribution with those concerned, but this is often a rarity. The appraisal interview may then be at best neutral in impact. Usually it is seen as a demotivating waste of time.

You may think this is not important – after all, those being appraised are more junior in the business. However, you also need to consider factors such as the sales you might lose through a demotivated switchboard operator who cannot be bothered to establish the right person a prospective customer might speak to.

Senior level

The problem may also exist at the senior level in a slightly different way. In the top two levels of your organization, how many of your directors and senior executives actually go through an appraisal process as appraisees and have points noted by way of actions?

There is the clearest correlation in my experience between how appraisal is supported in practice at the senior level and its effectiveness throughout the organization. Ultimately, the grapevine always ensures middle managers know the directors' attitude to appraisals.

In one company, a non-executive had been asked by the MD to have a "chat" with an already competent director "to help point the chap in the right direction", rather than go through an appraisal process. The recipient of this chat – over lunch at the golf club – was initially bemused at this strange and unannounced approach, and then angered. The moral of the story? Carry out the appraisal process properly, regardless of seniority.

Preparing adequately: what happens beforehand?

In the research that you or your adviser (if you have employed one – see page 46) carries out, you may well want to ask your managers and staff not only what help they receive in how to perform appraisals, but also what training they receive in related people-management issues.

Do not confuse explanations on what has to be done with how things should be done. One blue-chip organization, having been told by consultants that appraisers did not know what to do, proceeded to run two hour seminars about the appraisal form and how to fill it up. Both they and the consultants missed the point. The positive managers – and their staff – were actually saying "we've got these managerial jobs that we are trying to do well, but we could really do with some help to improve our management skills generally and our appraisal skills in particular".

So, as a rule of thumb, if you have staff who are promoted through the ranks to become managers because of their technical skills and are now managing "intuitively", then you may need to explore your whole approach to people management. Appraisal is part of that – it will become fully effective when managers are also coached or trained in people skills. In the real world, where management training does not always happen, a seminar about filling up the form may be of marginal help. But what you really need are guidance notes for all involved, clarification of responsibilities, and the availability of Personnel to help rehearse difficult problems. These issues are explored further later in the book.

Ask your staff

As you discuss with other managers and staff what actually happens during appraisal interviews and afterwards, you may find that managers are generally satisfied that they have done their best during the process in their role as appraisers. Perhaps that is what you would expect them to say. Ask the staff and they may give you a completely different story.

"I began to make a breakthrough in implementing appraisal when I carried out the first performance discussion ever with the technical director. We were both rather new to it, but the guidance I'd had beforehand was invaluable."
Managing Director

Common problems 2

When an appraisal process is not working all that well, these are often the common problems experienced:

- One or two key departments where everyone is "far too busy making money to bother with this sort of overhead activity"

- Inadequate prior thinking by appraiser and appraisee about their aims

- An interview that starts off with the appraiser saying "well, you and I both know that this is a waste of time; you know what I think of you and you know I have an open door policy, but I guess we have to go through with it".

- An interview that is in fact more like a monologue from the boss

- Concentration on all the appraisee's mistakes in the past year

- Concentration on how wonderful the appraisee is

- An absence of listening skills by the manager to establish the needs of the staff

- A postponed interview that is then interrupted by telephone calls

- An interview that is too short

- Training needs that are summed up as saying simply "you may need a course"

- Forms that are never fully completed or signed off

- Forms that are signed off by the appraiser's manager (the "grandfather") with comments that are different to the ones the appraiser has made

- Completed forms that do not relate to the interview comments

- Lack of clarity about who is responsible for doing what after the interview by way of follow-up action

- An assumption by the individual, manager and personnel that each will take the necessary further action to implement development ideas

- Explicit training and development needs that are not met within six to 12 months

- No review process after, say, six months, to check on progress

- Rapid filing of the forms by the personnel department without close analysis of training needs

- The loss of forms after a few months

- Annual salary review adjustments for performance that bear no relation to what has been said at interview

- Over 10 percent of completed forms where it is clear from the appraisee's comments after the interview that conflict with the manager is imminent

- Grievance procedures being invoked by staff because of the way the appraisal discussion is handled

- Discrimination cases at an Employment Tribunal using appraisals as evidence against the company

- A process that is amended each year because one director has an idea of the latest trends that in practice may not be relevant.

Active intervention

Does all, or some of this, sound depressingly familiar? If those responsible for the performance evaluation process within your organization check on what actually happens each year, then the specific problems that may be unique to your organization would become clearer.

These problems usually emerge within the first few years of the inadequate implementation of appraisal. They rarely get better on their own. You must actively intervene. The chief executive can take the lead in advocating change, perhaps responding to his middle managers who see the problems at first hand.

But the overhasty implementation of a "flavour of the year" (for example in the latest ideas on competencies) can simply worsen the problems at significant cost to the business.

Effective research and diagnosis of the problems should lead to workable solutions. It is important not to short-circuit the process.

Does the whole appraisal process make a difference?

Assume your appraisal process has been in place for five years. Most of the staff who have been with the company for that time have been appraised on average four times each, with between one to three different managers as appraisers as the organization has changed.

With average staff wastage, a whole new group of managers and staff will also have come on board and been through a couple of appraisal cycles.

Management aims

When launching the appraisal process five years ago, management probably had some aims in mind. You may have heard terms such as "aiming for total quality, continuous improvement, excelling in customer care, achieving a competitive advantage". You probably indicated that you saw staff as an essential asset that could be developed and that appraisal was a natural part of your human resources practice to ensure performance was monitored and improved. You may have used similar words since then when you have spoken to staff or delivered a session on an induction-training programme; or you may have left it to Personnel to do. So even if you have not had explicit links to your business strategy you have had some broad aims. Now you can check whether those aims have been met.

Costs

There has also been an annual cost for appraisal. At its simplest, the calculation may be quantified as the all-up employment costs of the preparatory, interviewing and follow-up time, perhaps averaging one to two days per employee per year. There is then the opportunity cost, as the cynical departments mentioned previously will tell you, when you could have been out making more money or providing a better service instead of doing appraisals. There are finally the costs of training or developing staff as a result of appraisal that are a short-term burden on cashflow, even though the company assumes that there will be a return on the investment.

Results

You may have been able to define outcomes for your organization and for key individuals because targets have been perhaps agreed at appraisal time. But what actually happened year on year? For example, did your more important senior people, who may have had weaknesses identified, improve? Were you able to win new business as a result of the need for advanced sales training that was identified in appraisal three years ago? And what happened to that fast-track executive where an individual development programme was established after discussion with him or her at appraisal time?

Even if some of the detailed outcomes are unclear, you may be able to ask yourself what would have happened to your people or the business in the last five years if you had not done appraisal at all.

Establishing what to do

Armed with all this data, you are now in a much better position to establish what has gone right, what has gone wrong and what your priorities might be as you revise the system. In particular, you may want to assess how it fits into your overall personnel policy and practice. If you, your colleagues and your staff are a bit uneasy about that policy, then appraisal may simply not work effectively.

In the rest of this chapter, we will help the manager who is new to appraisal assess his needs more carefully. You may want to glance at this section and the checklist at the end of the chapter. If not, move straight on to chapter three for the practical steps you can now take.

"It took a few years before the company linked performance review back to the department goals and forward to my own annual customer targets. Then the whole exercise began to make sense."
Key Account Manager

The proposed appraisal system

What are your aims in introducing a system?

Having read so far – and probably smiled at the pitfalls identified in the first part of this chapter – you clearly still want to proceed with introducing appraisal for the first time into your business. Before considering what you have to do and how you do that, it is as well at this stage to be absolutely clear in your own mind about your prime objectives.

As we have seen in the chapter one case study, the overhasty introduction of appraisal can lead to rapid demotivation of staff and exits of key people within the organization.

PRIORITIES TO CONSIDER WHEN STARTING APPRAISAL

In checking your intentions, let us be reasonably clear what the priorities are since they do have an impact on the design of the relevant process and the form itself:

■ Do you want to have a way of assessing performance so you have data that feeds into the reward process?

■ Do you want your managers to be able to give constructive feedback to their staff to try to eliminate their weaknesses and build on their strengths?

■ Would you like staff to be able to give upward feedback to managers?

■ Would you like appraisal to be one of the means of helping to deliver business goals?

■ Are you more interested in the personal development aspects for staff so that there is a focus on training and development needs?

You may feel that you have multiple needs. This is not a problem, but confirm this by consulting with your senior management.

Other factors

While you are still brainstorming, keep asking yourself:

- Whether planning for, implementing and following through appraisal will rank as a key operational project
- Whether there is time, money and resources to ensure success
- Whether you personally will be project champion and whether you can spare that time over some months, given your other responsibilities
- Whether you are prepared to set key success criteria that can be assessed one and two years on
- Whether you will be prepared for mistakes and learn from them.

You may be big enough as an organization to justify a Personnel function. Your Personnel Manager – through formal training and professional qualifications – should be capable of providing you with support and guidance to help take the project forward. But almost certainly, your role as a senior or middle manager is still absolutely crucial.

A fundamental question

The one fundamental question to ask is whether the organization is ready for appraisal. Like many other projects, there will never be an ideal time to initiate change, but the closer you come to having the ideal conditions, then the more likely it is that the project will be successful. So how do you know if you are ready? There are four crucial points to consider, discussed overleaf.

The proposed appraisal system

1. A vision for the future

Many companies have an instinctive dislike of forward plans. Successful because of their ability to think on their feet, business leaders believe that managing a budget over a period of a year is probably sufficient, given the speed of change and the need to think laterally to respond to opportunity.

Some leaders may express a vision for the future but do not necessarily translate it into specific goals, so that as an organization grows, and departments are established, other managers and their staff have a clear idea about what they should be aiming for. Even a few levels down in an organization, there can then be major misunderstandings and inconsistent activity. It is generally accepted practice that some form of forward plans for two to three years ahead, including broad assessment of the risks of proposed actions, is good practice. This strategy is endorsed by the leading employer bodies such as the IoD and CBI.

However, planning goes beyond pious aspirations or a wish list and has to be communicated effectively. It is also good practice to include in that plan a human resource element which addresses not only numbers of people, but also changing skill requirements.

Objectives

Since staff appraisal will almost certainly be based on some kind of assessment against individual objectives, it makes sense for those objectives to be linked to departmental ones; and for those departmental objectives to be geared to delivering business goals. So, for example, if one of your business goals is to open an office in Tokyo in two years time though a joint venture, and the sales targets for your merchandise are becoming clear, then the specific objectives for individuals might be explicit.

For one individual, this objective could be to learn a basic level of Japanese within 18 months. For another, it could be to consider and agree the advertising campaign with the joint venture partner.

Having a realistic business plan is one of the building blocks for good appraisal. As a minimum, there must be an annual departmental plan to which all staff in the department contribute.

2. Personnel policy and practice – how is it rated?

In an ideal world of a growing business, a Personnel Manager will provide the support you need. But what if you do not have a personnel policy in place yet? What might the warning signals be to put you off appraisal for the moment?

You might find that other managers are hiring their own staff and letting them go again within a year or so if they do not shape up. Your company secretary or lawyer provides a standard contract of employment, and action to terminate has always been taken within the period before an unfair dismissal claim is possible. But there is a constant turnover of staff that could be a concern. Are you getting to be the size where a Personnel Manager could help you? Should this be a priority? Appraisal will not work unless you have your fundamentals of personnel policy clearly established.

If you do have a Personnel department (and a staff handbook), how is the Personnel Manager rated by both managers and staff? What does Personnel actually do or be seen to do all day? Is it simply quoting the law at people? Does the head of the function sit on the top management table, and if not, why not? The Personnel /Human Resources function has not had a good press of late, partly because it is misunderstood, partly because it often seems to operate in a way that is divorced from business priorities.

Difficulties

If you do have a Personnel function that does not have credibility generally in the organization, or personnel policies that are divorced from reality, it will be difficult to involve the Personnel chief in developing an appraisal process that works. In practice, despite all the good intentions that you might have, the delegated responsibility for managing and administering the whole process of appraising staff will rest with the Personnel function.

The proposed appraisal system

"Face up to the problems, discuss them openly"

3. The competence of your managers on staff matters

Your managers have been promoted to their roles because of their technical competence, and you rate them as colleagues because of what they can contribute to profits. The effective research scientist ultimately produces marketable drugs; the sales manager wins market share; the corporate financier engineers the deal; and the solicitor gets the best deal for you.

No matter what the textbooks say, you do not mentally assess them on their people skills. In fact, the more technically successful they are, the less they seem to worry about their staff. For example, the partner in a professional practice may generate immense fees that impress his colleagues. However he may have a 100 percent staff turnover rate in his unit because he fails to delegate properly. This is a major cost to the practice, but is ignored.

If there are too many people like that in your business, appraisal is unlikely to work well, and could be a major demotivator. Many good Personnel Managers can tell you about the exit interviews they have carried out with competent people whose recent appraisals left them feeling hurt and undervalued. Managers naively thought the staff could improve by having all their faults listed.

So, if your colleagues at middle to senior management level are not rated for their people skills, training may be necessary. Postpone the appraisal until training has been carried out.

4. Actual training and development now

Most appraisal systems include discussions on training and development, and staff will have expectations that some training might be forthcoming. The introduction of appraisal, too, will itself require training.

If your organization is already committed to training and developing its staff to meet future objectives and actually carries out that training, you will be in a much better position to carry through post-appraisal action points. But if you are suspicious about the cost of training, do not have time anyway, and resent the period away from the real world of operational cut and thrust, then it is unlikely that you will see training and development as important. Your colleagues may feel the same.

Training investment

How much does your business actually invest in training? How does that compare with your competitors? There may be some rules of thumb. For example, large accountancy firms spend over 10 percent of their paybill on training their staff; and many organizations who see training as key to future competitiveness will invest more than two percent of paybill. Are you ready for an increase in the training spend that should almost certainly follow on from appraisal?

Have you begun to think about employability and personal skills development for staff that may not be fully linked to their job, but necessary to keep their skills up to date? This is the new "psychological contract", and some staff will want to talk about this.

CASE STUDY

In developing its approach to appraisal, a medium-sized company decided that it would be sensible to introduce a policy that encouraged its staff to spend some of their time and some of the company money on improving their personal skillsbase, so long as the education or training was potentially relevant. (Core-agreed training needs would still be funded by the company).

Staff with more than two years service were allowed a notional training credit of £500 per year towards the cost of a course or other learning event. Some spent this on relevant textbooks; others decided to work towards an MBA. All found it helpful to have advice and encouragement from their bosses at appraisal. Over two years, staff turnover went down from 20 percent to 12 percent, and recruitment costs were reduced as higher quality people queued to join. There was a rapid payback on this additional investment.

Those staff who were initially tempted by other offers at higher salaries discovered that the competitors did not have such an enlightened attitude towards training. They decided to stay with their current company and felt their future employability needs were being met.

Self-assessment

Before we move on to detailed planning for appraisal, it might be helpful to summarize the key points so far, so that you can assess where you are now. Give yourself a score out of 10 for each question, 10 being excellent, one being poor.

Notice that I have deliberately not used the word "appraisal" anywhere in this questionnaire!

	Question	Score
1	Do you have a reasonably coherent business strategy?	
2	Is it communicated to and understood by your staff?	
3	Do you have annual departmental plans that are communicated to staff and are based on the concept of continuous improvement?	
4	Have you carried out an audit of staff views in the last year formally or informally?	
5	Is your personnel policy and practice clear and rated as acceptable?	
6	Are you and your colleagues' management skills OK?	
7	Are they actually trained on appointment and their ability checked?	
8	Is your training and development activity as good as your competitors?	
9	Are you prepared to dedicate such time as is needed for the next year to champion and assist this project? Maybe five percent? Even if there are major operational crises?	
10	Do you have the real support of your colleagues at a senior level?	

Your Score

80–100

Implementing appraisal will be easy; your business is culturally attuned to the idea and it will work well; but do a quick double-check on your staff wastage and absence rates. If they are high then there could still be problems.

Of course, you may be optimistic by nature, so you should be certain that you are not kidding yourself. The more senior you are in a company, the more you may be unaware of actual practice in some of these areas. Ask a colleague to complete a questionnaire too, and compare results.

60–80

You have got a good start, but there may be issues you want to address in parallel.

Appraisal should not be considered in isolation, and there may be some areas of personnel practice that could be improved at the same time. You may, for example, have initiated a company communications policy last year, but the momentum gained then has since been lost. Staff will be cynical about another initiative if previous initiatives have not really worked all that well.

50–60

It could be worth considering postponing appraisal for a year while you deal with other priorities.

There may be quite important gaps in your human resources practice, even though you have scored highly in some areas. For example, although your senior colleagues like the idea of appraisal, it may be that their management skills are not yet at the required standard. It would be unwise for them to test their skills out for the first time during possibly difficult appraisal interviews with their staff.

Under 50

You may be underrating your company, or maybe you've had a bad week. If not, there are almost certainly some fundamentals that need to be resolved. Appraisal right now will not help. In fact, it could be counter-productive.

3

Starting your own system
Using external consultants
Getting what you want

Gaining your company's commitment
Action and development plan

Starting and improving your appraisal system

You are ready to get started; you have been through the analysis and are poised for action. You are moving from conceptual planning in principle towards more detailed planning. This is the next logical and essential stage. If you miss it out and jump to the specifics of implementation, you may go wrong.

What do you have to do, and how do you go about it?

In this chapter, we will consider those — important steps that come before the specific detail of the forms, the guidance notes, their introduction, and the follow-up. We will consider:

- How to gain real commitment from your colleagues
- The managing of a change process; project planning
- Consultation with all the interested parties at the sharp end
- The benefits of a taskforce approach
- The advantages and disadvantages of external professional help
- Timing in the annual business cycle
- Total communication.

At the end of this chapter it should be possible for you to draw up a personal action plan on the more detailed steps that are going to be necessary.

Gaining commitment at the top

With such an important procedure, it is likely that you will want to obtain formal agreement from the Executive Committee or its equivalent to introduce or reintroduce appraisal, even though you will have carried out soundings in the initial thinking stages. You may have already been asked questions by your colleagues such as, "how much is it going to cost?" and, "how long will it take?" Or you may have been met with the more cynical and worrying comments such as, "OK, let's get it over with" and, "yes I know John should really tell Fred about his lousy performance".

Your colleagues will have their own priorities and agendas, and unless they are exceptionally attuned to their staff, they are not going to be immediately enthusiastic at the thought of appraisal. Many may be sceptically neutral. Only a small minority is likely to see an appraisal system as a means to help enhance business performance.

So how important is it that you win their hearts and minds rather than simply their tacit agreement and gratitude that "somebody else is doing it?" Or worse still, how can you avoid the pitfall of their apparent support for you in return for your support at a later date for their own proposals?

Everyone must participate

Appraisal needs the full commitment of everybody on the senior team. Everyone needs to understand the potential benefits and the processes involved. Everyone, too, needs to be prepared to participate. More than one scheme has foundered because one of the directors was not prepared to have appraisal discussions with the four or five key direct members of staff who reported directly to him; when it came to the crunch, it was seen as neither urgent nor important.

The Chief Executive condoned this behaviour by not doing anything about it. The key managers could not be bothered to do appraisal with their staff so that the end result was that some 20 percent of the organization felt they couldn't be bothered. Once the rot started, it was too late to do much about it.

Get Personnel on your side

In another organization, two directors did appraisals, but felt that they were already so good that they skipped the training sessions beforehand. Their shortcomings were revealed when their staff started to leave a few months later. Remedying that was a major challenge.

If you do have the benefit of an effective Personnel function, getting them on your side at an early stage is helpful. The Personnel Manager can spend time with key directors and managers individually, listening to their concerns, and gently help to influence them so they realize that the time they themselves spend on appraisal is undoubtedly a worthwhile investment.

The outline paper that you then put to the Executive Committee should address all the issues, note the pitfalls, highlight some of the priorities or options and explore the benefits. None of your colleagues can then say in a year's time, "if you told me it would take the total of four hours per individual I would never have agreed".

Gaining commitment from the rest of the business

You have obtained the agreement of the top team. They say they understand the implications of appraisal and believe that it may be a bit of a challenge but they are prepared to learn. Hopefully none of them say it will be easy on the grounds that all their staff are brilliant anyway.

A further challenge now lies ahead. Your colleagues, the middle managers and staff who are at the sharp end of the business, winning customers, ensuring a competitive edge in practice and boosting your margins will be often both appraisers and appraisees. Do not assume that they will welcome appraisal with open arms. Even if they are attuned to the needs and aspirations of staff members, they may see it as yet another senior management initiative which has little relevance to their daily crises.

Their own staff – those who are in the engine room of the organization – will take their immediate cue from them. All too easily appraisal becomes labelled as yet another chore that has to be done because senior and middle management has said so. So winning the commitment of those lower down in the organization becomes as important as obtaining the support of the top people. Your middle management colleagues will be the ones who are likely to have to sell the new policy to staff such as junior accounts assistants and bought ledger clerks. Appraisal for these junior staff may seem irrelevant, so consistency in communication is needed. But before considering this later in the chapter, let us look at consultation first.

CONSULTING MIDDLE MANAGERS

In concentrating on consulting with middle managers, what do you consult about?

The options include:
- The best structure for the process and the details on the forms
- What unique objectives they might want to have
- The optimum timing
- The guidance notes and the nature of the introductory training
- The difficult people cases they might have
- Responsibilities during and after the process.

How do you best do this? Depending on the size of your business, it can be done either on an individual basis or through a small group.

The task force

As organizations become less layered and more consultative, there may be an opportunity to establish a small group of managers and staff who will be able to take forward your outline plan. The brief for this task force may be to seek views and opinions from others and put more flesh on the bones of the appraisal plan. It will need to have specific terms of reference agreed and be asked to deliver its findings within a set period of time.

If you work in a unionized environment, it will be essential to consult with the local representative. Culturally, it may or may not be right for him or her to form part of the task force, but he or she will almost certainly want to have some safeguards and press for all kinds of protection for members. It makes far more sense to confront and deal with these issues at an early stage rather than having to concede a point later simply to get the show on the road.

For example, some union representatives will want assurances about what happens if there is a clash of personality and one of their members is "unfairly marked down by a bullying manager". They may demand a right of appeal or some process that you may feel is unnecessary. If you can explain and consider with the representative the kind of introductory training that you are intending and the safeguards that will apply, they can be satisfied. Omit this step and there could be major problems later. Treating the union as a partner in this exercise is likely to be the most productive approach.

Representatives

In a non-unionized environment, the selection of staff members for a task force may be achieved through discussions with consultative committee members (who may themselves be suitable), or through identifying those who have made constructive suggestions about the business in the past.

The management members not only need to have enough interest and enthusiasm for the idea to make time for it, but also need to have sufficient credibility and weight in the organization to steer the progress of the group and fulfil its obligations within an agreed timescale. This may be done with the help of an external consultant.

Use of external consultants

If you have not thought about it before, it is at this stage in the planning process that you may begin to wonder whether the whole of the project is taking on a shape of its own that is eating up more of your time than you would ideally want.

It may also be taxing the skills of your Personnel colleagues who may have other day-to-day priorities. Your organization is theoretically "lean and mean". Additional workloads like this might be squeezed in, but what will be the actual benefits of the extra effort?

In addition, your own operational workload is probably heavy. So you consider whether you should buy in external help from consultants.

Costs of failure

Perhaps you are tempted. How can you begin to build up a cost justification?

The introduction of appraisal is a potentially sensitive issue that is emotionally charged. The actual costs of it going wrong in terms of reduced productivity or the loss of key staff are real. For example, the premature loss of

ADVANTAGES OF EXTERNAL CONSULTANTS

The advantages of external help for most businesses are likely to be:

- The purchasing of specific expertise based on a track record of the consultant's experience

- The provision of necessary additional staff to perform a task for which you do not have capacity

- The skills and objectivity of the external professional in taking soundings, leading a consultative process, and identifying barriers to change that might remain hidden to the insider

- Provision of introductory or updating training that has credibility

- A workable, tailor-made process that emerges as a result.

a competent manager who has been unfairly treated at appraisal will cost you at least six months' salary in replacement costs, loss of intellectual capital and customer goodwill.

Conversely, the good rating given to a performer who is no better than marginal, because the manager did not want to confront the issue and there was no professional assistance, followed by the individual's dismissal six months later can have potentially unlimited liability if the matter goes to an employment tribunal on discrimination grounds.

In the light of these factors, minimizing the risks will be important. Your time too is precious. Even freeing up two to three days from other project commitments could be important.

Moreover, you might take decisions that are unsustainable in the long term. So, having your own expert confidante could have its attractions. You will keep accountability but the chances of success will be increased substantially. And you should never underestimate the potential demands of your own day job as the business develops.

DISADVANTAGES OF EXTERNAL CONSULTANTS

The disadvantages of external help are well known:

- The consultants spend time at your expense learning about your business

- They may come up with obvious solutions that you could have thought of

- They do work that should be done by a competent Personnel function

- You do not have ownership of the process

- You resent the fees being paid and can think of better uses for the funds.

A constructive outcome

Maximizing the chances of a positive outcome from a new or revised process could be essential. You and your colleagues want appraisal to work and add value; you want a successful result not only in the first year, but all subsequent years. A good consultant increases the probability of a successful outcome.

The best time

If you do decide on external help, then you might want to work out the best time for involvement. Should this be before your paper to the Executive Committee? Or should this be at the consultation stage with other middle managers? It is unlikely to be later than that since the design of a process and the training depends on the introductory findings.

One option that you might consider is the consultant initially being part of the consultative process, and if appropriate, leading the task force.

So if the external cost is going to be, say, £10,000, you will want to be as certain as you can that you will achieve a payback by minimizing the risks and maximizing the chances of success. It is true to say that the majority of managers find that external help is useful. In addition to this, many organizations find that external assistance can sharpen their focus on best practice.

"We thought for a long time about the pros and cons of an outside consultant. After all, I had only recently hired an effective Personnel Manager and reckoned she could have helped get things going. But it was also time for the graduate milkround, and she was already working well over 60 hours a week, so, although she volunteered, it seemed better to get some additional help. As it turned out, the adviser discovered a number of other small, but growing, problems that we hadn't noticed. So we got value from the assignment."
Chief Executive Officer

CASE STUDY 1

A large successful financial sector organization felt that appraisal was not working very well. The Board was not entirely sure why, but one or two of the members felt that the evident solution was to introduce core, advanced and management competencies: people would then know what they had to do.

Commissioning external consultants to prepare a list of competencies, they were initially concerned to learn that the consultants intended to double check where the problems lay. They were then even more concerned at what they learned from the consultants' interim report of the results of confidential focus group meetings. These showed that the basic appraisal procedure was satisfactory but the implementation flawed and that neither the management nor the staff had received any training in how to manage the process properly. Competencies at this stage would therefore be a waste of time and would only have caused more dissatisfaction.

The procedure was tidied up to meet current needs, appropriate training run and outcomes monitored over two years. Consultation was started on identifying competencies with a view to full implementation by 2000.

CASE STUDY 2

A FMCG company had been considering appraisal over the years. One or two departments had moved ahead with informal systems and the Personnel Manager, in consultation with the CEO, felt it was time to rationalize the whole appraisal process.

An estimate of £5,000 worth of help by external consultants was seen to be too expensive. Because of other commitments, the new procedure took six months longer than expected and created some tension between departments. A compromise system was implemented which just about worked initially but fell apart in the following year when everyone reverted to what they were used to. Two graduate trainees left saying this was symptomatic of the business. Consultants were eventually called in to help sort out the problems at a cost of £7,500.

Selecting a consultant

Sources that you can use to hire a consultant include your professional body, non-executive directors, or your accountant or lawyer. The best source of all is a personal referral. It is important that the potential consultant understands the nature of your organization, has relevant experience ideally in both line and consultancy roles, and spends time asking you questions that might be awkward but necessary before finally submitting a detailed proposal.

Other requirements
He or she (and team if needed) should also be capable of gaining rapport with people at all levels in the organization and be prepared to come up with original and tailor-made solutions as appropriate after completing the appropriate diagnosis of the needs.

They will need to have had experience of introducing the relevant forms and guidance notes as wells as running support training. Finally, they must be able to transfer their own learning from their previous clients when completing the assignment. You may want to be able to draw on their expertise for some time, so investigate their aftercare service. Finally, award the contract on quality of potential service rather than just price.

The reality check and the business cycle
You and your colleagues work in the real world of operational cycles and the bottom line. You have budget targets to meet and departmental plans to implement, ideally within an overall strategy. You have to deal with internal and external customers, and get the best deal from suppliers. You refine, update and introduce new products and services. Even without an appraisal on your performance, you assess yourself against these targets and you are accountable for them to your colleagues.

Each week you are faced with the unexpected, but you know the times during the year when the whole enterprise is working at peak capacity to cope with both external demands as well as the demands of internal procedures. These peak times can include budgetary and statutory reporting deadlines, requirements from an overseas parent, or a new product launch.

When considering timing, remember also that you may want to use completed appraisals to provide some basic data that can help, for example, with salary and bonus reviews or with career decisions on filling key assignments. There will never be an ideal time but there will be times to avoid introducing and running appraisal. Near the year-end is a case in point.

Communication

If there is one issue that comes up time and time again in staff audits, it is the question of communication. Staff say they do not know what is going on or, worse still, have heard conflicting comments from different sources.

You may well have an established team briefing system with data about developments regularly communicated through departmental heads and team leaders. Alternatively, you may be using e-mail and internet facilities to ensure staff know what is going on to gain and retain their commitment. Or, alternatively you may still be developing a communications policy and currently just let staff know what is needed to help them do their jobs.

Whatever method you use, be sure to keep staff informed from the very early stages, especially when you either want their cooperation with representatives on a task force, or when your organization is of a size that there will be large numbers of staff who are not involved. And then every month, keep them updated with any developments.

Keep it simple

What you say can be kept simple. With executive committee approval, tell people what appraisal is, why you are doing it, what it means for them, and how the more detailed consultation is about to be done through a task force. If you have a briefing process in place, there may be questions that emerge that need to be answered promptly.

If you do not communicate effectively, nor use your middle managers to continue to convey appropriate messages, you may find that staff see appraisal in a completely negative way. This can happen even if you make changes in response to their comments and suggestions. They may be concerned that appraisal will be used as a way of criticizing people unfairly, dismiss it as just personnel-driven or be afraid it will be used as an excuse to hold down pay.

Rarely do staff who are left in the dark see appraisal as something positive. You and your colleagues need to work hard to win their commitment and keep them on side – getting that initial communication right will be surprisingly important.

"A good leader spends more time communicating than doing anything else. He must communicate with the employees to keep them all working towards the same goals."
Jan Carlzon, former CEO, SAS airlines

"*The only things to discuss are things that can be remedied or improved*"

Your personal action and development plan

Having thought through all the conceptual issues, you will have made progress in considering the initial stages of what you have to do. Before looking at all the alternatives and options that you might have in preparing the relevant documentation and launching the process (or in practice using your task force/Personnel Manager /consultant to do it on your behalf), you may want to review what you have done and learned so far, and more specifically, what steps you can personally take to ensure success as you move into the next phases. Simply answer 'yes' or 'no' to the following questions:

	Action and learning so far	Yes	No
1	Do I feel as certain as I can be that my organization is ready for appraisal or its relaunch? Do I understand what appraisal can be used for?		
2	Do we have the time, money and resources to dedicate to it as a project? How will it stack up as a priority against the other things we have to do?		
3	Am I aware of the sensitivities involved? Have I got senior colleagues on board and learned how best to handle objections?		
4	Have I considered how best to consult managers?		
5	Will I have an external consultant to help? Am I confident of getting the support I need?		
6	Do I now know how to communicate changes to staff? How will I achieve this?		
7	Have I begun to think about specific timing issues?		
8	Am I still keen and want to continue to be project champion?		

My action and development plan from now on

1. How will I now keep up my own learning on this during the detailed planning and launch phases?

_____

2. Can I make use of the external adviser to ensure that I am on track?

_____

3. Have I got a reasonable feel of the priorities my senior colleagues would like out of appraisal?

_____

_____

4. Is the task force with the consultant undertaking and completing its consultation effectively, and do I feel OK about ensuring we have a detailed project plan? Should I do that myself? Am I going to resist being pushed into launching appraisal too fast? Are the Personnel people making useful contributions? What should I do to ensure that we learn from each other?

_____

_____

5. When considering the options for the forms and elements of the system in detail, will I bear in mind the overall aims? How will I check out some of the detail with key executive members to ensure they are still on board?

_____

_____

6. Do I need to consider postponing the launch for a year if we hit problems?

_____

7. Should we operate a pilot system in one department?

_____

8. Will I make sure that I do the necessary pre-launch training myself so that I am at least an acceptable appraiser?

_____

9. Am I going to review my own performance as an appraiser carefully? And what about my own appraisal and future objectives with my boss?

_____

_____

10. Am I going to make sure we don't see appraisal as just a one-off for this year?

_____

_____

11. Am I prepared to see my inevitable mistakes as learning experiences and make next year's appraisal round that much better? How will I do this?

_____

_____

4

Alternative appraisal systems
Assessment ratings
Performance objectives

What to cover at an appraisal interview

The "grandfather"

Alternative appraisal systems and procedures

After you have completed all the consultation and planning stages, you are moving into the detailed implementation stage. As is usual in a project of this kind, you need to get the detail right.

In this chapter, we will look at alternative systems that you might want to consider and establish. Which one you choose depends on your priorities and objectives, and the views expressed by the task force, since you may want to include these in the consultation phase. In the next chapter we will consider what you have to do during the launch itself to ensure that appraisers and appraisees alike use the system effectively.

APPRAISAL FORM – THE IDEAL

Although the theoretical ideal appraisal form is a blank sheet of paper with no pre-conceptions about what ought to be discussed, in practice you will need to have as a minimum:

- **GUIDANCE NOTES FOR APPRAISERS**

- **GUIDANCE NOTES FOR APPRAISEES**

- **A FORM FOR BOTH TO COMPLETE.**

Simplicity

Simplicity in the choice of form is essential. Only if you have had successful appraisal in place for some time, would you want anything complex. The main concern that your colleagues will have is appraisal can take up too much time.

"I don't think our directors really understand the pressure we are working under at divisional level. Of course I recognize my people responsibilities and continually discuss performance and outputs, but doing complex appraisals properly and completing a 12-page form for my seven direct reports will take up twice the amount of time than a simple approach, with no added value for an organization of our size and culture."
Divisional Manager in an independent HR audit

Let's assume that you feel – as most employers do – that appraisal should cover a combination of assessment of performance against objectives, discussion of future performance criteria to meet agreed future objectives, and some consideration of future training and development needs. You may ultimately want to move towards a process that meets a specific priority, but you will be on solid ground if you initially keep to multiple objectives.

There are still some decisions to make, such as, should you have one policy and system for all levels of staff? We will address these queries in turn and consider the particular advantages or disadvantages of each one.

One form for all?

This may be a non-issue for a small growing business, but in medium-sized organizations you may ask whether the same appraisal process can apply right through the company from director to shopfloor worker.

The trend today is towards a uniform approach, and if in doubt you would probably want to adopt this policy. If you do, then the more simple the appraisal process will be, the more likely it is to work and help the organization improve.

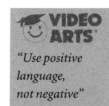

"Use positive language, not negative"

A STANDARD APPROACH

THE ARGUMENTS FOR A STANDARD APPROACH ARE:

- Everyone, even the cleaner, should have some agreed aims
- Everyone should aim to improve continuously
- You want a unified organization that minimizes the "us and them" syndrome
- You do not need to have a training requirement; it is sufficient to have a discussion with your manager about needs and the section on the form about training can be left blank if there are no needs at the most junior level
- You can add an additional insert if senior managers are, for example, going to consider competencies.

THE ARGUMENTS AGAINST A STANDARD APPROACH ARE:

- White collar and blue collar needs are different
- Blue collar staff may have different expectations and concerns and do not want long discussions on training
- The union will only support you if the form is different.

Assessment ratings and defining performance

Of all the contentious points that you will debate with colleagues, this is likely to be the most emotive. The majority of appraisal processes have historically had some kind of mark for appraisee performance, mostly on a five-point scale that is often defined using the words below. The descriptions used in each organization will vary, and some will have each of perhaps six tasks assessed with a score followed by an overall rating. This is what is meant by the phrase "box-marking" as used in the Civil Service.

APPRAISAL RATING OF 1:
EXCEPTIONAL PERFORMANCE that consistently exceeds all the requirements of the job over the whole year with no errors and a consistently more than expected contribution to the unit, department and the organization.

APPRAISAL RATING OF 2:
SUPERIOR PERFORMANCE that is substantially above the requirements of the job with minimal errors and a substantial additional contribution to the unit and the department.

APPRAISAL RATING OF 3:
FULLY COMPETENT PERFORMANCE meeting all the agreed requirements of the job, correcting minor errors rapidly; superior outputs in some areas will balance other marginally weaker outputs and continuous improvement is the norm.

APPRAISAL RATING OF 4:
NOT FULLY MEETING ALL THE AGREED REQUIREMENTS of the job; errors are more than would be expected and may be repeated, or agreed productivity targets are not met. A personal improvement plan is needed to achieve a competent performance level within six months.

APPRAISAL RATING OF 5:
FAILS TO MEET THE BASIC REQUIREMENTS of the job. Needs to improve immediately.

Dispensing with ratings

If you feel able to dispense with a ratings system, you will probably find on balance that you can cover the same ground and have higher-quality discussions through a combination of self-assessment by appraisees (see over) and good guidance for appraisers.

RATINGS – PROS AND CONS

There is a slow trend away from the ratings which are still used by many organizations.

The advantages of ratings are:

- Staff know where they stand
- There can be no lack of clarity
- There can be a direct read through to salary and bonus reviews
- Completed forms for above the norm performers can be useful for future development discussions
- Below par ratings may be needed for any subsequent disciplinary process.

The disadvantages of ratings are:

- Top down scores distract from the quality of discussion at interview
- Appraisers tend to give ratings of two or three, so that the distribution curve is skewed
- Some senior managers convince themselves that star performers "will always walk on water" or will leave the organisation if they are not rated as a one.
- Appraisers fight shy of giving poor ratings even when needed
- Appraisers in different departments interpret definitions differently
- Fully competent staff (which one would expect 70 percent of staff to be) nonetheless see themselves as just "average"
- It is psychologically difficult to "downgrade" an appraisee from a two to a three rating in the following year or on moving to new post even if it is justified and natural.

CASE STUDY

"I sat down with my new director for our first ever appraisal chat just after launch of the revised approach, and a lot of the discussion was initially reasonable as we considered what had happened in the last year. But then she started to talk about some marketing activity that the Board had apparently thought I had been working on and she wondered why I had not made any progress.

We then had a sterile debate for the next ten minutes while I had to convince her that I had no idea of what she was talking about. She eventually accepted my point, but the positive nature of the discussion had gone. At least we have now got agreed aims and six months on we are rebuilding an effective relationship. If I hadn't felt so committed, I think I might have responded to that head-hunter differently." Head of Division

Performance objectives

Most managers think they have a good feel for the key aims that they, together with their team, need to deliver. In a significant minority of cases, though, care has to be taken as appraisal is launched to ensure that staff's own views about the previous 12 months' apparent aims are noted.

Agreeing and setting objectives for the second year is a different matter. If one of your aims is to ensure that all staff have explicit objectives, then appraisers and appraisees need to consider jointly how far aims that are agreed can be specific, measurable, achievable, realistic and timebound (the acronym "SMART" is often used for this). As we will see, although these may often be reviewed half-way through the year, they can nonetheless be used as the basis for assessment in one year's time.

Much is written about the differences between objectives and targets. In practice, these are often blurred, and at this stage there is no need to confuse appraisers. Encouraging them to answer the question, "how will my staff and I know when the job is being done fully competently?" and to be explicit about it in consultation with their staff will, in practice, be sufficient. There may be four to six key objectives that are the main components of most posts. In this first appraisal round, the focus should be especially on the future and agreeing the key objectives for the following year.

Self-assessment

One of the most productive developments in recent years has been the use by appraisees of a self-assessment process. This helps appraisers significantly, since few managers really feel at ease with appraisal and would prefer to have greater input from below.

A typical self-assessment process will be based on a two- to three-page form for appraisees to complete before an appraisal discussion. The questions may cover an individual's views of their achievements in the past year, their strengths, areas for improvement, what support they would like from their managers in the future, and possible future development needs.

Could self-assessment help?

Given that you are adopting a new or revised practice, it would be sensible to consider whether self-assessment could help. It is often found that the input and thought provided by appraisees more than compensates for the feeling managers have that they may not be in control. Most managers welcome the large part of the agenda for the interview being flagged by the appraisee. In most cases, it helps them focus their thoughts, saves them time and is likely to provide a good basis for discussion.

Usually, the completed self-assessment form is given to the appraiser a few days in advance of the interview.

The advantages of self-assessment are:

- A sharing of the "burden" of appraisal
- Tangible input from the appraisee who provides much of the agenda
- A joint commitment to continuous improvement
- Honesty and often a harsher assessment of performance than a manager's.

The disadvantages of self-assessment are:

- Managers feeling left out of the process and abdicating their responsibilities
- Staff feeling that if they admit to weaknesses, it will be held or used against them
- Staff being uncertain as to whether the feeling within the company allows them to provide upward feedback to their managers
- uncertainty as to whether the self-assessment form becomes part of the formal record.

Timing and content of the appraisal interview

This discussion is central to the whole appraisal process. A poorly managed interview is likely to be a demotivator that is remembered by an appraisee for years afterwards. Conversely, the one that is well managed can prove a significant boost to morale and lead to a rise in productivity and commitment – even if the appraisee is a marginal performer.

One of the dilemmas you have to resolve is whether the interview should come after the appraisal form proper is completed or whether the interview leads to the completion of the form afterwards.

The advantages of completing the form before the interview are:

- Clarity of management comment
- Management control of the agenda.

The disadvantages are:

- The appraisal interview being somewhat sterile
- Debate about the words used rather than a constructive dialogue.

If you have reached the conclusion so far that some form of self-assessment is helpful, and that you want to be able to agree jointly some objectives, then it would be best to have the form completed after the interview.

What do you cover at an appraisal interview?

Managers and directors who for most of the year are fully in tune with the need to achieve a competitive advantage for the organization, and press home the fight in the external jungle, are sometimes reduced to quivering wrecks by the thought of an appraisal interview. Many a manager is delighted to find excuses not to carry out the interview. This same nervousness still applies even if managers have gone out of their way to give constructive feedback during the year, provide support and genuinely recognize the importance of managing people well.

The annual stock-take is nonetheless necessary as he or she knows, and nervousness is not called for. As in any other interview, the interviewer should talk far less than the interviewee and the main comments – even without a self-assessment form – should come from the appraisee. So the manager should set aside at least an hour at a mutually agreed time, keep to the interview time, and aim to get the appraisee to cover:

■ What went well and not so well, and why
■ How he or she might handle matters differently next time (the manager's input can usefully be added here to provide constructive comment)
■ What benefits he or she got from the training done in the past year

■ What SMART objectives might be agreed next year
■ What training and development might be helpful (see opposite)
■ What the manager can do to help the appraisee more effectively.

Praise should be given as needed since most people at all levels respond to positive feedback, and constructive suggestions on areas of performance improvement can sit comfortably with this. Notes should be taken so that the form can be completed after the appraisal interview.

If a self-assessment form has been used, then agreement should be reached on its use in the formal record.

Assessment of competencies

In addition to assessment of tasks, some organizations feel that it is helpful to assess and discuss the skills that are needed by staff to meet the requirements of the job. They can range from essential technical knowledge needs to specific core competencies such as analytical skill, adaptability, flexibility and management competencies, such as delegation. Descriptions are given of perhaps five levels in each competence and managers tick the appropriate boxes, or staff carry out a self-assessment. Learning needs can then be identified.

THE APPLICATION OF COMPETENCIES

The application of competencies can be helpful so long as all of the following steps have been taken:

1. Senior management are unanimous in their wish to use them, know precisely why, and can explain why to busy managers
2. A detailed analysis has been carried out by specialists on what is required to perform different jobs well to meet known business aims; these form the basis of competencies
3. Managerial skills are already at a satisfactory level throughout the organization
4. The appraisal process is already working reasonably well and has improved in its application over time
5. Continuous learning is an accepted part of the culture of your business and you are happy to pilot competencies in certain functions initially
6. The impact on other HR polices such as reward and promotion is considered.

If only some of these points have been addressed, you are not yet ready to use competency methodology. Keep everything simple for the moment. You can introduce competencies in a couple of years if you want.

Training and development discussions – the future

Part of the interview should include personal development plans, both short and long term. Appraisees may be glad to identify the needs they have to help improve performance, whether in the form of a course, or working with a particular colleague. It is essential that aims are clear and results checked.

Depending on the structure of your business, longer-term career development plans can be considered.

It may, for example, be mutually beneficial for individuals to gain experience abroad. Alternatively, a maternity leaver may want to consider options for a career break.

The employee comment

On completion by the appraiser, most appraisal forms are passed back to the appraisee for comment about the process and the agreed objectives. If an effective self-assessment process is in place, then the space required by an individual to add his views is usually small. However, it is important that the opportunity be given since any major differences in opinion should be aired. Then, and only then, the appraisal form can be signed off, showing that the procedure was effective, even if not all the comments were accepted.

The role of the "grandfather"

"I knew my performance was fine because my manager gave me good feedback during the year. But even though he had a sneaking suspicion (as he admitted later) that we had nothing to talk about at appraisal and that he was simply going to say 'more of the same', I found it really helpful to explore the overall direction we were going in and to consider openly my personal development. I don't think it was a coincidence that I exceeded my sales targets in the quarter following that interview."
Sales representative

Most appraisal forms have a space for comment by the appraiser's manager to conclude the process. This not only allows the so-called grandfather to see how well his or her managers are handling appraisal, but also allows a larger overview to be taken.

In a minority of cases, there may be a need for active intervention if there are extreme differences of opinion. So it is good practice for the appraiser to check out his with his manager in advance any appraisal interview and overall comment that may be at either end of the performance spectrum.

What happens then?

With the form complete, it is usually copied for appraiser and appraisee to review progress after three to six months, and the original sent to Personnel. It is important to know who has responsibility for the actions that follow. Typically, the employee ensures that training actually happens, the manager checks on progress against objectives and provides day-to-day feedback, and ideally Personnel looks at trends in the organization and acts as a reminder to all regarding actions. This will be explored further in the next chapter.

Guidelines for all?

At the beginning of the chapter we saw how it was important to have guidelines that would help both appraisers and appraisees. In practice, it can be most useful to have one set of guidelines that is available for everyone so that all parties know their responsibilities. The guidelines would normally be drafted by the external adviser and include all the relevant information outlined above, as well as details of some of the mechanics such as whether blank appraisal forms are available as a template on every computer.

The form itself

Once everyone has agreed what they want in, and from, the appraisal process, the design of the form follows on naturally. Rather than ending this chapter with a questionnaire, we can look at what a typical appraisal form might look like, taking into account what we have covered above. In the next chapter we consider the realities of introducing and running the process. Training will be of prime importance.

SELF-ASSESSMENT APPRAISAL FORM
Period: May 1998–May 1999

Name: _____

Department: _____

1. How do you feel you have performed against your objectives this year? What are your specific achievements?
_____
_____

2. What new procedures could have helped you perform your role more efficiently?
_____
_____

3. What are your strengths and weaknesses? How effective are you in your technical, personal, inter-personal (and managerial) skills?
_____
_____

4. What further support/training do you need?
_____
_____

5. What objectives in your role would you set yourself in 2000? What are your longer term aims?
_____
_____

6. Are there other points you would like to discuss at interview?

Please return this to your manager in advance of the appraisal discussion.

Signed: (Employee) _____

Date: _____

5

Running and evaluating the appraisal process
Training for appraisers
Training for appraisees

Keeping the channels open

Other guidelines

Questionnaire

Introducing, running and evaluating the appraisal process

Before you launch, pause for a while to consider what you have achieved and learnt so far. Remember, even with a fair wind, there will be, even now, enough people around in your organization who are going to find fault with a new or revised process. So a double-check is no bad thing.

DOUBLE CHECK Ask yourself:	Yes	No
1. Have I completed the consultation process and listened, through my task force, to key comments?		
2. Have I made rational choices about decisions, noting the views and comments expressed, so that I can justify them?		
3. Have business circumstances changed significantly since I first started considering this project? Do those make a difference?		
4. As I look at the time frame for the next few months, do I still have my colleagues feeling committed?		
5. If I have decided not to follow the external advice given by my consultant, can I justify my decision?		
6. Are senior management really going to dedicate the time and effort to develop their skills in appraisal over the next few weeks?		
7. Will they continue to sell the process to their staff?		
8. Have I made it clear that we may make a few mistakes in the first year and that we see appraisal as a continuously evolving process?		
9. Am I prepared to spend more time with my most sceptical colleagues to prevent them still feeling that, despite the progress made, this is just another personnel procedure?		
10. Are all the actual administrative procedures in place, or capable of rapid deployment, and has the task force considered all the immediate special cases such as staff on postings abroad?		

KEEPING THE CHANNELS OPEN

Perhaps, despite your best intentions, you have not got communication going. The options are:

■ The appropriate use of written communication methods, summarizing the history of the project, the rationale, the key findings and giving the detailed timetable. A note to all staff should come from the Chief Executive/MD to make clear the importance of appraisal clear.

■ A full two-week face-to-face programme involving you and the task force attending the main team briefings and discussing the implications of the appraisal project. If this attendance is seen to be at the request of the team leader it will be seen as a pragmatic, realistic approach.

■ In any briefing, even though you may well have covered them, the kind of questions that are likely to be asked include ones such as: "How does this affect my pay review?", "What do I do if I object to comments about me?", "Will this be used as evidence in a restructuring exercise?", "What training is available?", "Who's appraising you then?"; Consider your responses in advance.

■ A summary of the questions and answers raised at the briefing sessions can be drafted and subsequently distributed. Alternatively, if you have reached the final drafting stages of the guidance notes, the themes can be incorporated in the published version.

■ Deal with any special difficulties in timing that are caused by a multi-site environment or overseas staff by using direct communication.

■ Keep your union reps informed, especially if you are going to work in partnership with them.

Two main aspects

The two main aspects of a successful launch we will consider are communication and training – both essential and both much neglected; and then think about the whole evolutionary process over not just the launch period, but also over the next year.

Too often, management sees sending out the blank appraisal forms as the end of the matter and is surprised when the process later unravels. What you do in the next few months – before and after launch – can make or break appraisal in the medium term.

You do not want people to say in a year's time "that appraisal project was a waste of effort". What you want them to say is, "it really made a difference".

Communication

As the task force got going, it was useful to keep everyone in the organization informed of the overall intentions. You are now moving into the stages when you will find it impossible to spend too long on communicating. You should not underestimate the concerns, scepticism and potential hostility that may still exist in all levels of the business from just below the management hierarchy.

Senior management colleagues will have told their staff something about the project, but your latest 15-minute discussion with those colleagues may have been distilled into a one-minute briefing for their staff. Lower down the hierarchy, staff may have only been told "we've got to do appraisal soon".

Training for appraisers

"When the MD toured the country and visited the regions, he made the point of stressing the importance of the new way we were going about performance management, and included some time on it as well as the operating plan for the year. He made it seem like a perfectly natural thing to do, especially when he said a small team of non-execs would be looking at his own performance and considering his training needs".
Regional Manager

Most managers and staff will now know what is going to have to happen during the appraisal process. Few, if they are honest, will feel they necessarily have the skills to translate the "what" into the "how".

Yet the majority of new or revised appraisal processes in companies are launched with no training whatsoever for the appraisers, let alone the appraisees. As we have seen, such training as there is may take the shape of a workshop on the form, but it will cover what has to be inserted in the various boxes so that procedural obligations are met. It will probably not tackle the aspects of how best to do this and have a constructive dialogue with your colleagues. It will definitely not tackle some of the more challenging aspects of appraisal such as handling the marginal performers.

Let's be realistic about the time that busy managers as appraisers are prepared to spend learning about appraisal – unless your business is slack, forget the two-day course that has role-plays, CCTV, and theoretical models. At best, your company's managers may have been persuaded into a benignly sceptical stance about the benefits of appraisal but they may not be wildly enthusiastic. They will not willingly be prepared to leave their offices for a length of time to attend a course.

To run effective introductory or revision training for appraisers, you need a skilled and experienced trainer who has knowledge of your old and new appraisal

CASE STUDY

One of the most productive training sessions I ran with a group of senior managers in a business going through a process of upgrading its appraisal process was a 4.30pm to 6.30pm workshop. In it I relayed some of the findings from the task force, as well as the related HR audit I had carried out; showed the Video Arts *Dreaded Appraisal*; had some group work on best appraisal practice and considered the more challenging appraisals that attendees had to face.

After the workshop, I spent one-on-one time with the key people in the next few days ensuring that learning had taken place and rehearsing some of the individual problems they had. The knowledge they learned was thus transferred into potential skills. The whole process was evaluated after the appraisal exercise by a questionnaire.

processes (ideally this is your external consultant), a trainer who will identify overall needs, who will have credibility, provide an imaginative response, and run short concentrated programmes. In addition, your involvement as project champion is needed to introduce the sessions and to take part as a trainee. Some of the appraisers attending the training you provide will themselves be appraisees. They will be able to use what they have learned in a different context as they develop clear expectations of their bosses for their own appraisals.

Other points

There are potentially two other points that need to be covered in some detail in these training sessions – the phasing in of objective setting and the handling of marginal performers. You may also want to clarify points that have been made in the guidance notes on post-appraisal responsibilities and the six-month follow- up discussion.

Training for appraisers

1. Phasing in of objective-setting

Remember this is the first time appraisers are having to assess performance against objectives. In an ideal world, the most effective managers will have agreed objectives for their staff some months before as part of the normal day-to-day business operations, reviewed them as required and provided effective feedback on performance (whether or not formal appraisal is in place). But we are dealing with reality. And in the real world, most managers and their subordinates get by with fuzzy aims that fluctuate depending on operational crises, and with many managers making assumptions that all parties know what is required.

In this, the first year of the new appraisal process, it will be a rare manager that, with his staff, can reach a precise view about their outputs based on previously agreed objectives. While you hope that the introduction of appraisal will begin to focus people's minds, so that SMART objectives are now agreed and that next time round there will be a higher quality discussion, you cannot necessarily expect this in the first year. Indeed, many an appraisal process has got off to a poor start when appraisers have made critical comments about tasks that have not been done by subordinates,

when those individuals have had no idea that they were supposed to do them.

That is not to say that a constructive discussion cannot happen first time around. The self-assessment process can be based on actual achievements that are important and can provide a useful input into agreeing objectives for the next year. However a degree of ambiguity is to be expected initially.

In the training session, managers should practise how they are going to agree specific objectives with their staff.

2. Handling marginal performance

This is often raised by appraisers attending training sessions. It is always a source of concern.

Again, as with agreeing objectives, in the ideal world, most effective managers will have confronted marginal performance among their staff irrespective of whether or not an appraisal process is in operation. In the real business world, most totally ineffective performers are dealt with rapidly, but some marginal staff just get by – especially if their marginal contribution has been ignored for years. Many are unaware of their ineffectiveness as they tell everybody how busy they are. In a typical organization, I would expect at least 10 to 20 percent of staff to fall into this marginal performance category, perhaps justifying only 40 percent of their salary and other costs. That is a real loss to the firm that is often ignored.

Some of these staff are capable of improvement to meet a satisfactory standard with the appropriate guidance and retraining; others may not be and may ultimately need to be handled through the necessary disciplinary process (and perhaps leave).

Bringing the issue to a head

The introduction or revision of appraisal should bring the issue to a head. If the appraiser fudges now, you may have lost the opportunity to do something with a marginal performer for a long time. But if the appraiser feels, at the other extreme, he now has the opportunity to tell the marginal performer exactly what he thinks, in a non-supportive way, you may find that a lot of your future effort is spent defending your company at an employment tribunal against constructive dismissal claims.

Handling marginal performance for the first time is a skill that eludes most managers especially when some of the staff concerned may be long-serving and loyal individuals who may think they are doing their best in a changed environment. Great care is needed not to create more of a problem initially, and while it may be tempting to deal rapidly with the issue, a phased-in process is likely to be more helpful.

Individual circumstances

Since the circumstances of each individual case will be different, it may well be that in the training course only general principles can be considered, with each appraiser then seeking specific advice from his manager, the Personnel Manager or the external consultant in advance of the appraisal interview.

As a rule of thumb, it should be possible to have outcomes from a tactfully run appraisal with a marginal performer which has agreed standards of performance and targets, with appropriate remedial training, to be reviewed in three to six months. This can be backed up by a deferred salary rise. If the individual fails to respond and voluntarily resigns within six months, the cost to the business is likely to be less than that of an employment tribunal defence.

In many cases, of course, the marginal individual welcomes the clear guidance, responds well and becomes productive. Obviously, this is ideal.

Training for appraisers

3. Post-appraisal responsibilities

We have seen how important it is for appraisal to become a working process that is a clear part of the business, and provides an action blueprint for the future. The completed form, while eventually being filed, needs to be used effectively first.

Depending on the nature of your organization, it is worth stressing in the training session the respective roles of the appraiser, the appraisee, the "grandfather" and the Personnel function in the follow-up process. You will have covered this in the guidance notes, but it needs to be repeated. Many an appraisal action point, especially on identified training needs for the appraisee, fails to happen because nobody is entirely sure who is supposed to do what. By way of guidance, the trend is towards the appraisee reminding his or her manager about specific agreed action on training to ensure that it happens. The manager still retains the responsibility for ensuring that objectives are monitored and reviewed.

The function of Personnel should also be clearly defined. It may well be helpful in the training session for this role to be reinforced for information, and included in a handout, even though it might be outlined in the guidance notes.

Personnel checklist

Depending on its status and the size of the organization, this role can include, but should not be limited to:

- The full administrative process of despatching the blank forms and guidance notes providing ad hoc guidance to appraisers and appraisees beforehand
- Chasing completed forms
- Analysing overall trends
- Identifying company-wide training needs that could be resourced internally
- Identifying those staff who might be appropriate for developmental moves in any succession planning
- Ensuring the appropriate next steps are taken where marginal performance has been discussed for the first time with an individual
- Interviewing a cross-section of appraisees after appraisal as a quality check to identify improvements next time round.

4. The six-month review

The final point that needs to be covered in the training is what the manager should do to follow up progress on agreed objectives. In the fast-changing environment of most organizations, a formal check halfway through the year can prove invaluable. Some objectives may no longer be applicable; others may now need to be agreed; any major difficulties can be aired and feedback given. An effective trainer will go through with appraisers how best to handle a range of possibilities.

CASE STUDY 1

"I initially thought this training would be a complete waste of time; after all, anyone can do an appraisal, or so I thought. In fact, each of the four appraisals I had to do was so different and was so much harder than I thought.

One test was that both my staff and I felt good about the real appraisals. I guess I used at least half a dozen tips I picked up from the training. This included some questions I asked my staff to help improve my management style. It was also vital to follow up the reviews a few months later. With one of my people, it was clear that the original aims were already out of date."
MANAGER, INSURANCE COMPANY.

CASE STUDY 2

"Having recently been appointed to the board, it seemed odd that as champion for the whole appraisal project, I was strongly advised by the external consultant to attend the training sessions. I felt I must know more about the subject than most, but I went along anyway. Some of my fellow directors had to be dragged along. One said he hated these 'group grope sessions'.

I actually learned quite a lot. The most valuable part was the syndicate discussion that the consultant ran for the board at the end of the second day. That was when my colleagues and I – including the sceptics – discovered how, in practical terms, agreeing objectives and evaluating performance could be applied at our level. Even my most cynical colleague could see the idea. That was progress. In retrospect, that session put appraisal on the business agenda."
MARKETING DIRECTOR

"Common sense is unteachable only in the sense that it isn't learned overnight. A fool doesn't wake up one morning a sage. But even the most foolish person over time can become significantly less foolish."
Mark McCormack, CEO, International Management Group

Training for appraisees

If you have adopted a self-assessment process (see chapter four), then some guidance for future appraisees can be invaluable before launch. Although still unusual, giving some advice to those at the more junior end of the organization on how to make the most out of the appraisal system can help. This is more likely to be in the form of "handy hints", than any skills practice, and to build on the guidance notes. It can be done in large groups for short timespans by the personnel function or by the consultant. As project champion, your attendance for a few minutes to introduce the sessions will add credibility.

WHY BOTHER WITH APPRAISEES?

■ Appraisal is designed to be of mutual benefit to employer and employee

■ Staff need to have a major input into the process to make it work effectively

■ Staff are often more critical of their own performance than their bosses, but can also identify some of the more detailed achievements that bosses might have overlooked

■ Their appraisers are not always skilled in managing the interview, and are likely to welcome questions such as, "how do you feel I could have done that task differently?" as a prompt to encourage constructive comment

■ Staff are likely to complain out of management earshot about the awfulness of appraisal if they feel excluded.

The timetable at launch

This will depend on the size and complexity of your organization. You will already have spent perhaps six months in the initial planning phases and are now into the detail of the launch. Your administration timetable is likely to look like this:

LAUNCH MINUS TWO MONTHS: report of the task force/external consultant and agreement on the structure of the forms and guidance notes; communication update

LAUNCH MINUS ONE MONTH: sign off on the forms and notes for printing, plus additional communication/briefing visits and invitations to future training for appraisers and appraisees

LAUNCH: distribution of all forms and guidance notes; templates on computers as required

LAUNCH PLUS 1 DAY to c.2 WEEKS: carry out all the training for appraisers and appraisees

LAUNCH PLUS 1 TO 2 WEEKS: difficult cases rehearsed

LAUNCH PLUS 2 TO 6 WEEKS: all self-assessments and appraisal interviews carried out

LAUNCH PLUS 4 TO 8 WEEKS: completion of the forms and return to Personnel

LAUNCH PLUS 2 TO 4 MONTHS: analysis of outcomes by Personnel and data available for management; final chasing of outstanding forms

LAUNCH PLUS 2 WEEKS TO ONE YEAR: carrying out of agreed appraisal action points such as training and development

LAUNCH PLUS FOUR TO EIGHT MONTHS: follow-up interviews by appraisers to review objectives and consider progress on difficult cases

LAUNCH PLUS TWO TO EIGHT MONTHS: your evaluation of outcomes and consideration of appropriate adjustments to the process for next year (see below)

WITHIN SIX TO EIGHTEEN MONTHS: the inclusion of any large-scale outcomes in your organization's next business and HR plan.

"If you're not planning where you want to be, what reason or excuse do you have for worrying about being nowhere?"
Tom Hopkins, author, *How to Master the Art of Selling* .

Training for appraisees

If you feel that a detailed critical path is going to be needed, then you may be right. Appraisal is as major a project as your new product launch.

Evaluation

Like any other major project, your post-project audit of outcomes will prove essential in your quest for continuous improvement. Although you will have aimed high, there may be lessons you and your colleagues can learn from the inevitable mistakes.

If you managed to agree four or five key objectives for appraisal beforehand, then you will be in a good position to start to check whether these objectives have been met within two to three months. Since some of the objectives are longer-term ones, such as individual development assignments, it may be a while before you can reach a coherent conclusion and report back to your senior colleagues. Some of your views will be based on perceptions, some on actions.

You can start, of course, with the return of the completed forms within the deadline of the exercise. Not an end in itself, an overall return rate is nonetheless one way of verifying interest. A success rate of over 80 percent is very good; anything under 50 percent means that you need to go back to the drawing board (and get rid of your consultant, too!).

Delays

You can then check initial reasons for any delays. Even though you may have chosen a launch time in the business calendar that looked sensible, Murphy's law suggests that if anything can go wrong, it will. One department will have a crisis caused by factors outside their control, perhaps involving suppliers or key customers. Another will find its technology going down at a crucial time. Or perhaps your US parent will ask your MD to fly to the States at short notice for urgent discussions on an unexpected acquisition opportunity.

Sounds familiar? Appraisal will not be the only project that gets delayed in some units, but it is important – unless you are on your deathbed – that you, as project champion, complete your appraisals on schedule if at all possible. One well-known globetrotting troubleshooter is occasionally forced to carry out appraisal interviews with his number two in a quiet area in a business class airline lounge. Not something you will find in the textbooks, but a pragmatic solution.

When evaluating outcomes, all the wrong signals will be given for future years if the appraisals you are doing on your own staff are delayed. But you will be able to reassure others about the genuine reason for delays on other projects elsewhere in the business.

Other evaluation guidelines

To conduct your analysis objectively, you may want to use a combination of the Personnel function, an external consultant and you. Your decision on actions to take will depend on the outcomes, but do not be afraid, for example, to run additional training or retraining for appraisers next year if required. Alternatively, you may feel that it has all gone so well that you can begin to consider the more advanced aspects of appraisal such as competency development or more formal upward feedback mechanisms – so long as the business case is clear.

Normally, there would be a strong case to retain the same forms and process over at least two complete cycles and only change the process at the margins, unless your evaluation has shown up some appalling outcomes. In the second cycle, correct the mistakes made the first time round. Aim for changes in small bites only.

Before we move on to the final chapter of the book and consider some of the more complex aspects of appraisal and future trends, let us check to see where we have reached.

You have read up to this point in the book and then gone back through each chapter as you have planned, consulted, launched and evaluated the whole appraisal project.

Let's assume it is now a few months after launch and you are evaluating all the outcomes.

OTHER EVALUATION GUIDELINES

The other tools you can use, depending on your objectives, are:

- Discussions with the heads of department, as appraisers and "grandfathers", to consider the quality of the forms that they have seen and the usefulness of the action points
- Questionnaires at selected levels to judge the usefulness of the training and the benefits of the process as a whole
- The usefulness of the information for salary review and succession planning purposes as judged by the relevant committees
- Verification after about six to nine months on the percentage of the agreed action points in the forms that have been implemented (more than 70 percent would be very good given changing objectives during the year at the individual level)
- A check that there are, after a reasonable time, clear outcomes on the marginal performers and other difficult cases
- A check that there is good-quality data for medium-term business and people planning purposes.

Questionnaire

1. Looking back at my personal development plan at the end of chapter three, how far did I manage to meet my objectives? What were the specific challenges? Are there going to be any barriers to continuous improvement remaining in the future? If so, what will I do about them?

_____

_____

2. How did I get on with appraising my own staff? If it was more difficult than expected, what did I learn? How close was I really to an example of best practice?

_____

_____

3. What have I done about all the follow-up actions?

_____

_____

_____

4. Have I actually had the follow-up discussions with my staff to ensure that the objectives agreed then are still OK?

_____

_____

_____

5. Have I maintained momentum on day-to-day performance discussions with my staff so that I have not left it all to next appraisal time?

_____

_____

_____

6. How did my own appraisal go? Have I maintained responsibility for ensuring that some of the outcomes actually happen?

_____

_____

_____

7. When studying the overall return rate and quality of appraisals in the firm, have I identified operational units where quality standards might have slipped below what I would expect? What will I do about this?

_____

_____

8. Have I thought through the content of the review paper I will need to put to my management colleagues shortly to plan for the next appraisal round? If asked "was it worth all the expense?" what will I say? How can I show the benefits?

_____

_____

9. What should the priorities be to underpin continuous improvement in appraisal as the organization changes?

_____

_____

_____

10. As new senior managers come on board, how am I helping them learn about appraisal?

_____

_____

_____

11. What are new staff being told about appraisal at induction?

_____

_____

_____

12. Have I had value from the external consultants? Have I reviewed outcomes with them and provided feedback? Since they have learned a lot about us, will they be of future use? Or can we do everything ourselves from now on?

_____

_____

6

Future trends
Multicultural companies

The networked telecommuter

Questionnaire

Future trends and emerging issues

This chapter will help you consider some emerging themes and related issues that are likely to be important in the next few years, or could be appropriate in certain circumstances. Some issues will apply more to larger organizations than to others, but as companies increasingly deal with external competition on a global scale, leading-edge responses will be needed to maintain people competitiveness. Effective appraisal has a role to play within good human resources practice.

Some caveats

However, there are some caveats. If you have been developing an appraisal process and have incorporated the advice in the first five chapters, the first part of this chapter will be more relevant when you have a record of success over a couple of years. It will also be relevant if you are in a particularly complex organization that is rapidly evolving and perhaps restructuring. Nonetheless, your business needs are paramount and the points in this chapter should not be considered in isolation. Some may be intellectually interesting, but it would be unwise to adopt them without an analysis of their benefits to your organization right now.

360 degree appraisal

This is jargon that is often loosely used to mean upward feedback or feedback from colleagues to managers. In the chapter five case study, a manager asked specific questions of his staff in appraisal to obtain feedback on his management style. In the majority of businesses this is likely to be sufficient, so long as the manager is receptive. The questions need to be open ones and the manager needs to act on the input from staff. "How can I change the way I do things to help you?" is a more productive question than "I am sure that everything I do is OK, isn't it?"

In some businesses, a manager's own appraiser will spend some time with the manager's staff to obtain overall comments about management style in advance of the appraisal interview, and may also speak with key customers and colleagues. This is best practice and often a good option.

In a minority of organizations, an external consultant is sometimes brought in to interview a manager's subordinates against some pre-agreed competencies and provide anonymous feedback. This may be done around appraisal time. When introduced by bullish senior management to shock apparently poor middle managers, this rarely works well. On the other hand, when introduced, after consultation and professional analysis of the management competencies, to help a broad range of already effective managers to become the best around, it can be powerful. If in doubt, seek advice.

Competencies

These have been mentioned earlier. You may have been tempted to incorporate them in the appraisal process but have probably deferred consideration until you could be certain they would help. One good test of whether they would help is to see if your senior colleagues raise the idea with you first. Alternatively, your regulatory body may propose them.

Establishing core, advanced and managerial competencies that are going to be useful requires professional help, through the use of structured interviews with individuals and focus groups to identify what is needed to make people successful. Since it has an impact on other aspects of human resources policy such as reward, the approach needs care and a significant investment. The investment can be worthwhile: a successful business using competencies well is likely to be more productive than the norm. Competencies work best when they are seen as a way of encouraging continuous improvement and self-development, rather than yet another way to tell staff they are good or bad. Thus, training activities can be successfully built round competency development, generated through a self-assessment process.

Outputs

Nonetheless, if you are still keen to move down the competency route in the future, you need to be careful not to forget that outputs from a job and the ways staff carry out tasks are likely to be just as useful as the inputs in the shape of competencies. So, for the assessment of a sales professional or key account manager, should a sales director spend some time finding out from the customer how the salesman comes across face-to-face (an output), or spend time assessing if he can be flexible (an input)?

"Change is the law of life. And those who only look to the past or present are certain to miss the future." Former US President, John F. Kennedy

CASE STUDY
"Appraisal had gone OK in the first year, and better in the second. I was considering some innovations for the third year, but realized that 20 percent of the organization was completely new and that we were beginning to change strategic direction. I spent time talking with the Board, and it was clear that there was no need for a new policy just for the sake of it. Gradual evolutionary change was better." Personnel Director

Emphasizing future development and quality standards

You may have introduced and run appraisal with multiple objectives and have done so successfully. There may be one future trend, however, that you need to note. In some organizations, especially in the technological sector, corporate goals are revised every few months. Managers become effective in agreeing frequently changing objectives with their staff and providing ad hoc feedback and guidance.

Such staff, too, may not necessarily see their long-term careers in the same organization, and perhaps four to seven years' service may be of mutual benefit. They may be especially interested in keeping their skills up to date. In some organizations, groups of staff are employed on two- or three-year fixed term contracts, and before accepting an offer they will be particularly keen on knowing what development is on offer. In these circumstances, a formal classic annual appraisal begins to seem a bit of an anachronism.

An alternative

One alternative is to concentrate more on the developmental aspects of appraisal so that there is a short, relatively informal meeting every six months between boss and subordinate that helps set up and then monitor a Personal Development Plan for the individual. This plan considers the types of work assignments or attachments that might be of benefit; the coaching that might help from the manager or colleague; the courses or conferences that could be of benefit or broaden interest and knowledge ; further education that might be relevant in the long term; lectures that might be delivered or articles written.

In some circumstances, an innovative company (as we saw in the earlier case study) might agree an individual learning account of a few hundred pounds each year plus a certain number of days for developmental training over and beyond what is required for the immediate job. The sums invested are returnable if an individual leaves prematurely.

Avoiding replacement recruitment

As a retention device within an imaginative overall training policy, this approach is cost-effective. Experience shows it keeps your better people motivated and avoids unnecessary replacement recruitment since they tend to stay longer.

Testing out a revised process through a pilot in one department is one option for you to consider.

Remember that getting the right appraisal process in place at the right time is not just best practice. It becomes a major foundation in any externally verified quality drive such as Investors in People or the European Quality Standard.

Appraisal and Investors in People (IIP)

IIP is a business improvement process that helps ensure that your staff are effectively trained and developed to meet your business goals. Established for nearly a decade and involving over a third of the UK workforce, IIP accredited organizations often report better morale, higher productivity and profitability.

The fact that you are interested in constructive appraisal means that IIP might be a logical next step for you to consider. Or, if you made a commitment to IIP a few years ago that fizzled out, then ensuring appraisal really works will probably help you regenerate the process.

With four well-tested principles, and 23 detailed indicators to act as a checklist, IIP can be usefully deployed as a way to ensure you move towards good practice standards. The principles ensure that you:

- Adequately plan for the future of the business and communicate your strategic aims to all your staff
- Commit to training and developing your staff throughout their careers
- Carry out the training as agreed
- Evaluate it effectively at macro and micro levels so you can demonstrate the benefits.

Using appraisal first

Since good appraisal is central to training and development as well as essential for delivering business goals, I have found with clients in all sectors that getting the appraisal process right over two to three years means they are perhaps two-thirds of the way towards achieving their quality aims. Successful IIP assessment then follows with much less difficulty, not as an end in itself, but as an externally verified quality standard. You can proudly show this to all actual or potential stakeholders in your business. Success then breeds success.

In practice, for example, you may meet some of the IIP indicators in the second year of a new appraisal policy that allows staff to review the benefits of training in the previous year. Staff can then plan training and development more effectively with their managers for the following year.

IIP is now increasingly being considered as a helpful tool outside the UK since its principles are perceived to be universally valid. You may want to contact your local Training and Enterprise Council for more information.

The networked telecommuter

As organizations grow and evolve, there are an increasing number of staff who work outside the office on a near-permanent basis. This is especially the case in IT, where systems staff can work away from base, and maternity leavers who might work from home. There are also "virtual" call centres that consist of electronically linked people who might rarely meet.

Their appraisal and development is, of course, an integral part of effective communication and management. Successful appraisal processes may require a degree of imagination to implement but are arguably even more important to ensure a shared understanding of both business and individual goals.

If your business is changing like this, face-to-face consultation with the individuals concerned is undoubtedly a good starting point.

Seconded staff at home or abroad

The argument for a simple appraisal process is reinforced when you have some of your staff seconded to other organizations. These organizations may be government bodies, overseas parents or multinational joint ventures. Their managers and directors might need to make use of your forms and guidance notes for the seconded staff, or you will need to conform to what they do on appraisal. For a period of a couple of years during a secondment, you might be flexible about the process so long as the essentials in appraisal are covered. Clarity and communication as to what you as the seconding body need is useful at the start of the assignment.

It can be helpful for the individual secondee to have the opportunity to talk with you as the parent organization at least each year. You (in practice the head of the seconding department) can use the completed form as a basis for discussion. That way, you will at least cover the training and career development issues and check that action is taking place. The reverse of course applies to staff seconded to you.

Emerging categories of staff: their appraisals

You may well find that an increasing number of the staff in your business are in practice employed on a long-term temporary basis through a third party agency, or are self-employed contractors. These are not individuals who work the occasional day or week, but have specific skills that may be in short supply, and have a long-term relationship with you.

Sometimes, given inevitable future business uncertainties, it may be that you cannot yet reach a decision whether these people should become permanent staff. Quite often, they do.

The arrangements are of mutual benefit. You pay them a premium over ordinary staff in return for keeping the official headcount figures down, for the ability to fire them at will and for not including them in your usual benefits package. In practice, the total additional cost is quite small and their contribution is essential as they develop a knowledge of your business and its products. In the best organizations, they become indistinguishable from permanent staff.

"I suppose this is one slightly more refined variant on the temporary to permanent regime that we have deployed at a secretarial level over a number of years," one Personnel Manager told me. "We could certainly not manage our continuing IT projects, for example, without contractors, and once these people have been here for six months there is a mutual investment in continuing success. So I guess we somehow need to look after them."

Should you appraise them?

Should the contract staff who do stay somehow be included in the appraisal process? Conventional wisdom is they should not, but you may want to re-assess the situation from time to time if these scenarios arise:

■ In any department, contract staff have been employed for more than six months and there is a likelihood they will be needed for a similar future period

■ In any department, they make up more than 30 percent of the headcount over a six-month period

■ Some investment in their development may be of mutual benefit

■ Even after they leave you, you might want to call them back from time to time to assist, and you want them to give you priority when there are bids from other organizations

■ Your overall appraisal process has been running successfully for two years, and you could consider a significantly modified form for them.

The multicultural entity

Setting up and developing an appraisal process in a one-country environment may be a manageable challenge. Devising and developing a procedure that will work across nationalities and take into account implicit, but not necessarily explicit, cultural agendas is another matter. For example, the British trend towards openness in appraisal is not shared in the Far East where a top-down hierarchical management style is more common. On the other hand, Scandinavian nationals will expect to give significant upward feedback to their managers.

So what do you do if you find that you are the appraisal champion in such an environment where the working language is English? You may need professional advice at an early stage since the pre-launch phase will be longer and more complex than in a national environment.

Mergers and acquisitions

The impact of a merger on an existing appraisal process is probably never considered in pre-merger discussions. This is not surprising since human resource policy and practice is rarely considered at the right time anyway during negotiations. Although appraisal may not be at the top of the agenda, try to avoid the imposition of one system on the whole merged organization, unless you are a larger acquiring company with a good appraisal process swallowing up a small one without appraisal. Even then, you need to remember the training required for participants.

It is advisable to go through the analytical stages first as described above. A new appraisal process that takes into account the revised goals of the merged organization can prove a powerful unifying tool.

"The merger we completed last year did not go smoothly, not least because, I suspect, we did not consider our human resources policies until quite late. Fifteen months on, my Personnel Director has persuaded me that a new appraisal process would better reflect the changing vision and values of a larger company, and I expect we'll launch it in a few months time." **CEO**

CHECKLIST FOR MULTICULTURAL APPRAISAL SYSTEMS

1. Establish precise shareholder expectations, what the organization's goals are and how they are articulated

2. Try to establish a vision and a common set of values that all the top team feel comfortable with (they will often express these in the form of desirable behaviours)

3. Get a feel for the cultural barriers that are impossible to shift (probably fewer than you fear)

4. Communicate the vision and values to staff

5. Clarify business priorities for the next two years

6. Clarify departmental and individual goals

7. Devise a workable appraisal process that meets the essentials in year one, including compliance with local employment and data disclosure legislation. It can be refined over time, and perhaps take three rather than two years to settle down

8. Be prepared to spend more than expected time in training appraisers and appraisees off the job and building an agreed policy and practice within an emerging human resources policy.

Final questionnaire

1. When considering amending or upgrading your appraisal process, have you taken into account all the organizational, regulatory, legal, international and multicultural issues that are likely to have an impact on what you are doing both now and in the next year or so?

_____
_____
_____
_____

2. Have you got an effective human resources policy and are you operating within it? Does it need to be adjusted to cope with change?

_____
_____
_____
_____

3. If you feel that you would like to be imaginative and innovative, is this coherent with your type of business? Why? Can you pilot your ideas in one unit first?

_____
_____
_____
_____

4. If you set the pace in your sector, what efforts will be needed to maintain the momentum and then evaluate outcomes?

_____
_____
_____
_____

5. If you are considering quality standards, what part will appraisal play?

_____
_____
_____

Remember Jim?

Lastly, remember the case study in chapter one on Jim, the entrepreneurial MD who introduced appraisal in his IT company with such disastrous results? Have a quick look at it again. And then answer these questions:

1. **What preconditions were in place for successful appraisal?**

2. **What planning took place in consultation with his colleagues?**

3. **What steps did he take to win hearts and minds?**

4. **What training did participants have?**

5. **What evaluation was carried out?**

And the answers...

1. None

It does not seem there was a clear business strategy or departmental goals, and Jim's people management style was excessively autocratic. He needed to spend time on these points first and to begin to review the performance of all his colleagues, but perhaps only the non-execs could have pointed this out and discussed his style with him.

2. None

There was no consultation, and the use of a previous form was a recipe for chaos. What would you have done instead?

3. None

The tacit acquiescence of his colleagues reinforced his mission.

4. None

There can never be an assumption that an entrepreneur who has been successful so far will intuitively know what to do to meet good practice standards in a structured and partly bureaucratic process such as appraisal.

5. Some

Jim was not stupid. He recognised in due course that his apparently brilliant idea was a disaster, and spent the next two years rebuilding the business with some more explicit strategic goals and delegated responsibilities. With initial reluctance, he took a month out at a business school and followed this up with personal coaching to modify his style.

After 18 months, he felt he had a new mission – to get appraisal right, and took all the appropriate steps to launch it. Three years on, the business had a major competitive edge in its market and was achieving externally verified quality standards.

Index

Further reading

DTI and DfEE, *Competitiveness through Partnerships with People,* (1997)

Institute of Directors, *Partnerships with People* (1998)

Heller, *The Essential Managers' Manual,* (Dorling Kindersley, 1998)

Bruce and Pepitone, *Motivating Employees,* (McGraw-Hill, 1999)

The FT Handbook of Management (Financial Times, 1999)

Maslow, *Maslow on Management* (Wiley, 1999)

Munro-Faure, *The Success Culture,* (Pitman, 1996)

White, Hodgson and Crainer, *The Future of Leadership,* (Pitman, 1996)

Kamp, *Successful Appraisals in a Week,* (Hodder and Stoughton, 1998)

Gillen, *The Appraisal Discussion,* (Institute of Personnel and Development, 1995)

CONTENTS

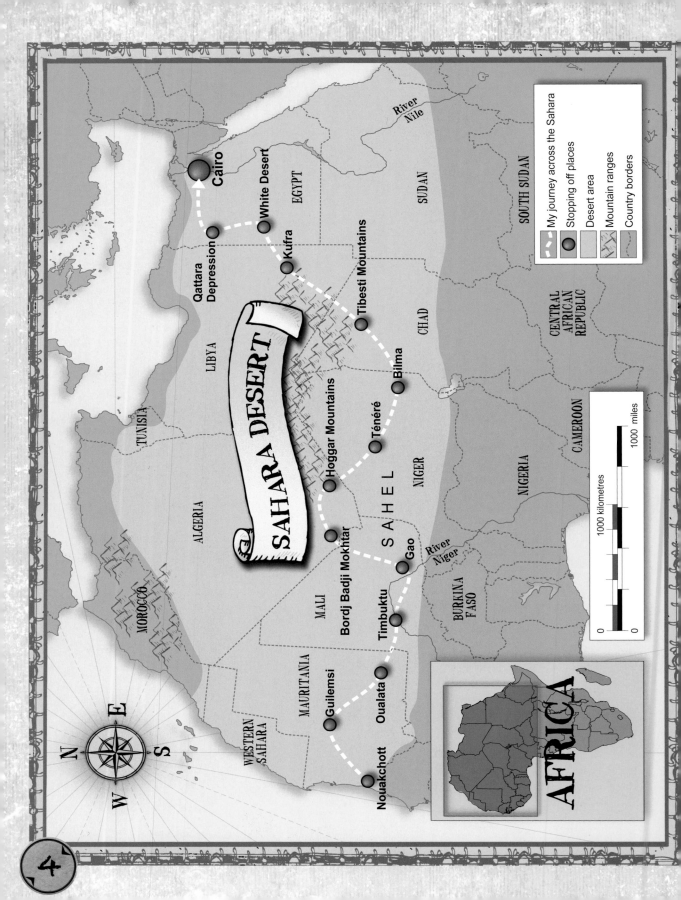

SOU

Published in paperback in 2017
by Wayland

Copyright © Hodder and Stoughton, 2017

ISBN: 978 0 7502 9860 5
10 9 8 7 6 5 4 3 2 1

Wayland
An imprint of
Hachette Children's Group
Part of Hodder & Stoughton
Carmelite House
50 Victoria Embankment
London EC4Y 0DZ

An Hachette UK Company
www.hachette.co.uk

www.hachettechildrens.co.uk

A catalogue for this title is available from
the British Library

Printed and bound in China

Produced for Wayland by
White-Thomson Publishing Ltd
www.wtpub.co.uk

Author: Sonya Newland
Designer: Rocket Design (East Anglia) Ltd
Picture researcher: Izzi Howell
Map: Stefan Chabluk
Wayland editor: Elizabeth Brent

Picture credits:

P5 Nickolay Vinokurov/Shutterstock;
P6 mtcurado/iStock; P7L Nature Picture
Library/Alamy; P7R N Mrtgh/Shutter-
stock; P8 Necip Yanmaz/iStock; P9L
hagit berkovich/Shutterstock; P9R Anton
Ivanov/Shutterstock; P10 oversnap/iStock;
P11T Ibrakovic/iStock; P11B Quick Shot/
Shutterstock; P12 Quick Shot/Shutter-
stock; P13T PatrickPoendl/iStock; P13B
Richard Whitcombe/Shutterstock; P14
Imagemore Co., Ltd/Corbois; P15T
Chantelle Bosch/Shutterstock; P15B
KarelGallas/iStock; P16 Pichugin
Dmitry/Shutterstock; P17L quickshooting/
iStock; P17R Nigel Pavitt/JAI/Corbis; P18
Paul Harris/JAI/Corbis; P19T RosaFrei/
iStock; P19B Kurt Drubbel/iStock; P20T
Milene123/iStock; P20B Pavel Szabo /
Shutterstock; P21 Pavliha/iStock; P22
age footstock/Alamy; P23 Stefan Thüngen/
Wikimedia; P24 mariobono/iStock; P25
cinoby/iStock; P26 PRILL/Shutterstock;
P27T Universal Images Group/DeAgostini/
Alamy; P27B Michael S. Lewis/Corbis; P28
Joel Carillet/iStock; P28T Anton_Ivanov/
Shutterstock; P29B LucVi/iStock.

THE SAHARA DESERT

Preparing for the trip

I'm so excited! On 16 October I set off on the journey of a lifetime across the amazing Sahara Desert (see map opposite). These days lots of people explore the Sahara in a four-wheel drive, but I'm starting with a more traditional form of transport — camel! This is one of the harshest landscapes on earth so I'm prepared for some tough going, but I'll have a guide for some of the way and I've been training for months. I'm ready!

The greatest desert

At 9 million square km, the Sahara is the largest dry desert in the world. It stretches across the whole of North Africa, from the Atlantic Ocean in the west to the Red Sea in the east. This vast desert blankets parts of 10 countries — Mauritania, Morocco, Algeria, Mali, Niger, Tunisia, Chad, Libya, Sudan and Egypt — and the territory of Western Sahara.

Climate

To survive in the Sahara, timing is everything. In the winter months, the temperature in the desert can drop below freezing at night, and ice can even form. At the height of summer, daytime temperatures can soar to a deadly 40 °C. There's also a higher chance of sandstorms in the spring. Rain is rare in the Sahara — on average there's only about 2.5 cm of rain a year. Some parts of the desert can go without rain for 10 years or more.

Equipment

I've decided to bring along the following:

- hat
- walking boots
- long trousers
- first aid kit
- map and compass
- sun cream
- tent
- torch
- matches
- sunglasses
- binoculars
- sheet of tarpaulin
- signalling mirror
- water bottle
- sleeping bag
- whistle
- strip of muslin

30 October
Nouakchott to Guilemsi

Well, I've certainly learnt a lot in my first couple of weeks in the desert! I met up with my guide – and my camel – in Nouakchott and we headed straight off into the wilderness. We travelled north-eastwards towards the heart of Mauritania because I wanted to see some of the rock paintings here at Guilemsi. This amazing ancient art is proof that people have made their home here in the desert for thousands of years.

Much of Nouakchott's population is nomadic, living there for a while then moving on.

Nouakchott

Mauritania is a country on the western edge of the African continent. Fifty years ago, Nouakchott was little more than a fishing village, but when Mauritania gained independence from France in 1960, Nouakchott was chosen as the new capital. Since then, it has developed into a small but thriving city near the Atlantic Ocean. Droughts have caused many people to move here from surrounding areas, which has contributed to its growth.

Be smart, survive!

The first few days riding a camel were hard work, but my guide gave me some tips to make things easier. Wearing long trousers is essential to stop your legs getting chafed and sunburnt. There are no stirrups on a camel saddle, so don't grip tightly to its sides, let your legs hang loose. Take a break every few hours and walk around so you don't get too stiff. Most importantly - relax and enjoy the ride!

Saharan landscapes

The part of the desert we've been travelling through is sandy, but not all of the Sahara is like this. Huge stretches are made up of bare rock and gravel. There are also high ridges and plateaus, as well as mountains. Across the width of the continent are oases, where towns have been built and plants grow around rare water sources.

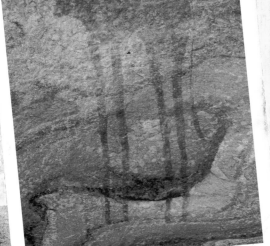

Guilemsi

At Guilemsi, about 50 km north of the town of Tidjikja, runs a long sandstone ridge. On rocks, boulders and the stone walls of dry riverbeds all around are ancient paintings. Some are simple handprints but others show scenes with people and animals such as horses, antelope and cattle. Around 200 km east of here is more evidence of early desert dwellers — the Tichitt culture. The remains of walls and other structures suggest that there were many Stone Age settlements in this area as long ago as 2000 BCE.

DESERT MAMMALS

1 November
Guilemsi to Oualata

Back in Tidjikja I said goodbye to my camel. I have a long way to go and I need a quicker form of transport now – a four-wheel drive. As I headed towards the small town of Oualata in south-east Mauritania, I saw herds of antelope and heard the calls of the jackals far in the distance. It got me thinking how amazing it is that animals can survive here, in one of the harshest environments on earth.

Camels

Centuries ago, Oualata was an important stop on the trans-Saharan trade route. Merchants would rest here with their camel caravans loaded up with goods to sell. Camels have long been the traditional form of transport for Saharan people and they are well suited to desert life. Their fatty humps mean they have a store of energy to burn when they can't find food in the barren desert.

Screwhorn antelope

The screwhorn antelope, or addax, is one of many types of antelope that roam the desert. It's also the largest indigenous (native) mammal in the Sahara. Sadly, the addax has been hunted almost to extinction for food and for its beautiful horns. With only 500 left in the wild, it is now critically endangered.

Fennec fox

As I was setting up camp last night, I spotted one of the desert's best-adapted animals — a fennec fox. These small mammals spend the sweltering desert days underground and come out at night to hunt. Their large ears help them to locate their rodent prey, but importantly they also carry heat away from the fox's body to help keep it cool. Their thick fur also protects them from the sun and keeps them warm during the chilly nights.

Desert dangers

The desert may look empty, but it's actually filled with life — and not all the animals you'll find here are as cute and harmless as the fennec fox. Before you set off into the desert, find out what sort of creatures you're likely to encounter. Take a book along with you to help identify any animals or insects that may prove deadly!

GET OUT ALIVE!!

CITY CULTURE

4 November
Oualata to Timbuktu

I've now crossed the border into Mali, and yesterday I finally arrived in Timbuktu, one of the few large population centres within the Sahara. I love camping in the desert, but it's great to be in a city again – to be among crowds of people and to spend a night or two in a proper bed! I've had a great day exploring this fascinating ancient city.

Women walk along the sand road past the Sankore mosque in Timbuktu.

Timbuktu

Timbuktu lies at the southern edge of the Sahara, near the River Niger. A settlement was first established here in the fifth century, and by the fifteenth century the city had become a great centre of Islamic learning and culture. It was also an important commercial hub, as people came to trade in ivory, salt and slaves. Today, the city is a World Heritage Centre, famous for its rich history and its amazing architecture.

Religion

Most people in Mali — and across the Sahara region — are Muslims, although there are also populations of Christians in some North African countries. Long ago, Timbuktu attracted many Islamic scholars. The Arabic word *Madrasah* means 'place of learning', and there are plenty of these in Timbuktu. Three great mosques remain from the city's heyday: the Djingareyber, Sankore and Sidi Yahia. Together these make up the University of Timbuktu, which was founded more than 1,000 years ago.

Be smart, survive!

Always be aware of the dangers of the sun and the heat. Carry a water bottle with you at all times and drink from it regularly to stop yourself getting dehydrated and falling ill with heatstroke or sunstroke. Avoid travelling in the midday heat and whenever you're outside, cover yourself with sun cream and wear a hat.

Buildings

I've noticed that the architecture in Mali is very unusual. A lot of buildings are made from mud-brick — sandy soil mixed with water and straw, then moulded into bricks using a rectangular frame. This ancient method of construction can be seen in the great mosques of Timbuktu as well as homes and other structures in the surrounding area. Sadly, many of the beautiful buildings in this part of the Sahara are under threat from desertification.

DROUGHT AND DESERTIFICATION

17 November
Timbuktu to Gao

I chose to get back on a camel for the journey to Gao, around 300 km from Timbuktu. As I travelled slowly along the route of the River Niger, through the southernmost part of the Sahara called the Sahel, I saw for myself the many environmental problems that this region is facing.

For the people who live in this part of the Sahara, the River Niger is a vital source of water and transportation.

Water sources

Some boundaries of the Sahara are marked by water sources, including Lake Chad in the south and the Red Sea in the east, but water is scarce in the desert itself. The River Niger and the Nile in Egypt are the only two permanent rivers in the Sahara. In some places, however, water can be found just below the surface, along stream beds that stretch out from the mountain ranges. Deeper underground there are huge layers of rock filled with water, called aquifers.

The Sahel

The Sahel is the region between the arid desert parts of the Sahara and the savannas that lie to the south in sub—Saharan Africa. Human activity has caused many problems here. People have cut down trees so they can farm the land and graze livestock, but this has caused desertification and soil erosion. Global warming means that droughts are more frequent and last longer than before. This part of North Africa once supported both people and animals, but it is becoming increasingly difficult for either to survive.

Be smart, survive!

It's not easy to find water in the desert. If you need to search for a water source, climb to high ground and use a good pair of binoculars to search for valleys, as you're most likely to find water in low-lying areas. Also look out for birds and animals, which are good at finding water in even the driest environments.

Vehicles used by tourists are damaging some parts of the Sahara.

Flash floods

It's tempting to make camp in the dried creek beds known as wadis, as they can offer some protection from the wind, but this isn't a good idea! Rain may be rare in the Sahara, but sudden downpours can cause these old creek beds to fill up faster than you can get away.

GET OUT ALIVE!!

13

DEADLY CREATURES

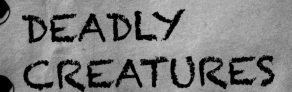

8 December
Gao to Bordj Badji Mokhtar

I've finally reached a small commune on the Mali–Algerian border. It was a long trek to get here, but it's really helped me to hone my desert survival skills. Making camp one evening, I noticed a creature scuttling across the sand and realised it was a deathstalker scorpion. Desert animals don't have to be big to be deadly!

Scorpions

The deathstalker is one of the most poisonous creatures in the desert – a sting from this large scorpion would be extremely painful at best and at worst it could kill you. These, and other species of scorpion, are well-adapted to the desert environment. They get all the liquid they need from their insect prey, and some scorpions only need to eat a couple of insects a year to survive.

Be smart, survive!

Before I climb into my sleeping bag at night, I always check it carefully for creepy-crawlies that may have sneaked inside. The same applies when getting dressed in the morning – I give my clothes a good shake before putting them on so I don't get a nasty bite from an insect that's made its bed in there!

Some snakes bury themselves just beneath the surface of the sand so you can't see them clearly.

Snakes

Sidewinder snakes are common in the desert. I haven't seen a real snake yet, but I've spotted the tracks in the sand caused by their sideways slithering movement. Among the deadliest desert snakes is the horned viper, but there are many others, including huge pythons that crush their prey. In fact, nearly 100 different species of reptile make their home in the Sahara – lizards and tortoises as well as snakes.

Monitor lizards

Prehistoric–looking monitor lizards can grow to be nearly 1.5 m long! These venomous, meat–eating reptiles hunt other creatures such as rodents and insects. They can be aggressive towards humans, especially in the cold season, so it's best not to approach one if it crosses your path.

Snake checks

There are several poisonous snakes in the Sahara, including vipers and adders. To avoid getting bitten:

1 Watch where you're walking – step onto rocks and logs instead of over them.

2 Never harass a snake – many of them will attack you if they feel cornered.

3 Before you set up camp, use a stick to turn over rocks in your campsite to check no snakes are hiding underneath.

GET OUT ALIVE!!

DESERT PEOPLE

26 December
Bordj Badji Mokhtar to the Hoggar Mountains

I've ventured deeper into Algeria now, to the Hoggar Mountains. This range of peaks runs along the Tropic of Cancer, the imaginary line around the Earth halfway between the North Pole and the Equator. Here I've been able to spend some time among the Tuareg tribe – one of the highlights of my trip so far!

The Hoggar Mountains.

The Tuareg people

The Tuareg are a nomadic people who live across the southern Sahara in parts of Algeria, Niger, Mali and Libya. Like other indigenous people of the Sahara, the Tuareg are herders. They live in tents so they can move quickly and easily when the land is no longer any good for grazing. As they move around, the Tuareg visit the market places in oasis towns and villages to trade their livestock.

The Blue Men

Tuareg women do not cover their faces but Tuareg men wear veils. I was lucky enough to witness the 'first veiling' of an 18—year—old man. This takes place in a special ritual performed by a holy man called a marabout, who reads from the Qur'an as he winds the veil. The veils are made of a cloth dyed with indigo, so the Tuareg have become known as the 'Blue Men of the Desert'.

There are around 350,000 Toubou people living in the Sahara.

Be smart, survive!

It is important to keep the sand out of your eyes and keep your head cool in the glare of the sun. A long strip of muslin, around 2-3 m, can help you do both these things. Wind the muslin loosely around your neck and up over your face, covering your nose and mouth. Leaving just a slit for your eyes, keep winding it around your forehead and build it up more tightly over your head.

Other desert peoples

There are other nomadic tribes in the Sahara. The Sahrawi people live in the Western Sahara and Morocco — in fact, their name means 'from the Sahara'. The Toubou (Rock People) inhabit the Tibesti Mountains of northern Chad and southern Libya. They are divided into different clans, who live in semi—permanent settlements around water sources in the desert.

PLANT LIFE

Aïr and Ténéré Nature Reserve

The Aïr and Ténéré Nature Reserve is one of the largest national parks in Africa, covering parts of the Ténéré Desert and the Aïr Mountains. Here in this World Heritage Site I've been able to see an amazing variety of animals, including addax and other endangered antelope. The water reservoirs in the mountain valleys allow plants such as acacia and palms to flourish here.

30 December
Hoggar Mountains to Ténéré

In the bustling town of Tamanrasset I picked up a vehicle again for the next stage of my journey. It was a long drive over the border into Niger and right into the heart of the country. I've set up my camp here in a stunning nature reserve among the Aïr Mountains.

Desert plants

In general, the lack of water makes it hard for plants to grow in the desert, but some hardy species can be found in the Sahara. Acacia, palms and shrubs grow low to the ground and have long roots to reach underground water. Occasionally wild flowers can grow in the desert after a flash flood, but they are usually short-lived.

Catching water

Even in the dry desert, dew forms in the morning. If you need water, stretch out a sheet of tarpaulin on the ground or tie it between trees or even tents before you go to bed. It will catch the morning dew and provide some drinking water in times of need!

The lonely tree

In the Sahara here in Niger there was an acacia tree known as the 'Lonely Tree of Ténéré'. It was the only tree for more than 400 km, and it provided welcome shade for merchants with their camel trains for over 300 years. It was able to grow because there was an underground well right by its roots. Sadly the tree was knocked over by a car in 1973, and all that stands in the desert here now is a memorial to the lonely acacia!

SAND SEAS

1 January
Ténéré to Bilma

I've learnt that scorpions and a lack of water aren't the only dangers the Sahara holds. As I headed deeper into the desert from Ténéré I found myself caught up in a sandstorm, which was an incredibly scary experience! It's a great relief to be lying here now under a clear sky, staring at stars that seem almost within touching distance, among the incredible sand dunes in the Erg of Bilma.

Different deserts

The name Sahara simply means 'desert' in Arabic. The Ténéré Desert is just one of many deserts within the vast Sahara, and they have several different features. Much of the El Djouf Desert in Mauritania, where I started my journey, is covered in rock salt. The Tanezrouft Desert, spanning parts of Mali, Algeria and Niger, is thousands of kilometres of barren sandstone plains.

Ergs

I'm currently camped in the dramatic landscape of the Erg of Bilma. This is one of many ergs — vast areas of sand dunes that are constantly being shifted by the wind — in the Sahara. The loose, slippery sand makes ergs tough terrain to cross, but the dunes are brilliant for some extreme sports, including sandboarding and racing dune buggies!

Ergs are 'sand seas' – huge stretches of sand where nothing grows.

Be smart, survive!

Dry winds are common in the desert. They don't all cause sandstorms, but they can still make life uncomfortable if they blow sand around. When planning your campsite, try and pitch your tent on the leeward side of sand dunes, as this will offer some protection from the winds.

Sandstorms

Desert winds can catch particles of sand or loose soil and whirl them all up off the ground to create a sandstorm. These may build into huge storms that engulf large areas. In some places the storms can take all the rich topsoil off the land, which makes it hard for plants or crops to grow. Sand can travel great distances in a storm – Saharan sands have even reached the UK!

Sandstorm danger!

GET OUT ALIVE!!

If you see a sandstorm coming, try to find some shelter, but don't keep moving when the storm strikes. Visibility can be almost zero – you may not even be able to see the sun and you'll certainly lose sight of any landmarks that might be helping you to navigate.

It's better to stay where you are until the sandstorm passes so you don't lose your way.

DESERT PEAKS

5 January
Bilma to the Tibesti Mountains

My next stop was Mount Koussi on the southern edge of the Tibesti Mountains, in Chad. I've grown used to the variety of landscapes that the Sahara has to offer, but as I stand here on the edge of the crater, looking out to the panorama beyond, I have to say this is one of the most dramatic places I've visited on my trek. The vast emptiness of it all makes me feel very small!

Saharan massifs

More than a quarter of the Saharan landscape is covered in mountains, or massifs. The impressive Atlas Mountains stretch for 2,500 km across the northern edge of the desert in Morocco and Tunisia. The mountains of the middle Sahara, where I am now, are actually the highest points of a rocky sandstone ridge that runs right across the continent. Deep gullies in the Tibesti Mountains are evidence of three great rivers that flowed here thousands of years ago, when the desert climate was more humid.

Mount Koussi

I caught a lift with a cargo truck heading out towards Mount Koussi – there aren't many roads here and it's best to travel with someone who knows the way! It's worth the detour, though. This volcano is the highest peak in the Sahara, at 3,415 m. Koussi is now extinct and no one knows for sure when it last erupted, but some experts think it may have been two million years ago! It's possible to walk to the top of Koussi to wonder at its huge crater, which is 19 km across and 1,200 m deep.

Be smart, survive!

It can get cold in the mountains at night, so I build a camp fire to keep warm. The fire also warns off any wildlife that might think about getting too close! I gather up dry sticks and pile them into a pyramid shape. If I can find dry grass I put some in the middle to help the fire light. I've kept my matches safe to make sure I can always light my camp fire!

Signal for help!

GET OUT ALIVE!!

I've brought a signalling mirror with me on my desert adventure. If I hold this up and move it around, it will catch the sun and make flashes of light that can be spotted up to 60 km away. This will help attract attention if I get lost in the mountains – or anywhere else for that matter!

OASIS LIFE

11 January
Tibesti Mountains to Kufra

Back in civilisation at last! I'm spending a few days in the Kufra oasis in Libya to rest and recharge. I'm also keen to learn what life is like in these busy settlements, which seem almost like mirages among the dry desert sands. It really is amazing how green everything is here compared to the barren mountains and desolate plains I've travelled through!

What is an oasis?

An oasis is an area of vegetation in a desert that grows up around a water source. The trees and plants are able to thrive because underground aquifers in these areas carry water close to the surface. This also means that people can dig wells to access the water, so settlements grow up around them just as they do along the banks of rivers.

Know your plants

GET OUT ALIVE!!

Many plants and trees around oases provide edible fruits that you can munch on if your food supplies are running low. Look out for olive trees, date palms and delicious figs. You might also find a doum palm, whose fruit tastes like gingerbread!

Kufra oasis

The Kufra oasis in Libya is in a dip called the Kufra Basin that lies over a series of huge underground reservoirs. There are freshwater lakes here, surrounded by palm trees and other vegetation which were planted to protect the water from being polluted by sand carried by the wind. Kufra is part of a project to develop agriculture in the Sahara by running pipelines from the area to drier parts of the desert.

Market traders

For hundreds of years, oases have been important stops for traders and travellers — and they still are today. All oases have busy, colourful marketplaces. I spent some time in the market at Kufra, watching the traders buying and selling their goods and livestock such as goats and camels. I'm surprised by the sheer numbers of people, in particular the many migrants from southern Africa, who stop off here on their journey to Europe.

25

SAND SCULPTURES

18 January
Kufra to Qattara Depression

My amazing desert trek is nearly over. I've crossed into Egypt – the last country I'll be visiting – and I'm about to set off to explore the Qattara Depression. I took a bit of a detour to get here, though, because I'd heard about the incredible sand formations in the White Desert further south and I didn't want to miss my chance to see them!

The White Desert

So-called because of its chalk-white landscape, the White Desert is a national park and one of the Sahara's biggest tourist attractions. People come here to see the strange formations dotted across the desert landscape like giant mushrooms. These wind-formed sculptures make me feel like I'm on another planet — especially when seen by the light of my flickering camp fire.

Be smart, survive!

The glare of the sun off the desert sand can seriously damage your eyes. Symptoms can simply be your eyes feeling sore and gritty, but in extreme cases the glare can cause a temporary blindness. To prevent this, wear good sunglasses - preferably wraparounds for fuller protection. If your eyes do start to feel sore, cover them with bandages and rest them until they improve.

Qattara Depression

I've visited the highest point in the Sahara and now I'm in the lowest — the Qattara Depression, which lies 133 m below sea level just over 300 km west of Cairo. This vast, barren dip is filled with salt marshes that stretch for 300 square km across northern Egypt. They eventually meet up with the dune-covered Great Sand Sea.

Salt

The Qattara Depression isn't the only part of the Sahara where salt can be found. Trade and industry in the regions were built around the availability of salt, which was mined and sold across North Africa and beyond. Salt is still mined in the Sahara, including at the Fachi mines in Libya, and salt caravans can still be seen crossing the desert.

JOURNEY'S END

22 January
Qattara Depression to Cairo

I've arrived at my final destination - the bustling city of Cairo, capital of Egypt. However, before I catch my flight home after my epic adventure, I just have time to experience the sights, sounds and smells of this ancient settlement. As I wander through the streets, I think about how amazing it is that such a busy city thrives in the desert.

Cairo

Cairo is the largest city in the Sahara and it is absolutely packed with people. 22 million people live here, and thousands of tourists visit every month to admire the nearby pyramids and explore other remains of ancient Egyptian culture that lie further afield. The roads are filled with cars and a heavy smog hangs in the air, but despite this, Cairo is an attractive and energetic city and I enjoy wandering the streets, listening to the shouts of the market traders.

River Nile

As one of only two permanent water sources in the whole of the Sahara, the Nile is incredibly important to the ecosystem here. The river runs the full length of Egypt and eventually flows out through the Nile Delta into the Mediterranean Sea in the north. The annual flooding of the Nile makes the land on its banks very fertile, so crops can be grown.

Save the Sahara

Today, pollution and overfishing are having an environmental impact on the Nile. Seeing this makes me think about the environmental issues facing the whole Sahara region. Because the desert is so dry, people tend to crowd into the less arid regions on the edges, but this is causing huge problems. If we don't address these issues soon, the people and animals of the Sahara will be lost.

Be smart, survive!

I can't do much to stop the overpopulation in areas like the Sahel, but global warming is also causing problems there and I *can* do my bit to reduce that. When I get home I'm going to start using public transport and walking more. I'll also try to save energy around the house by switching off lights and gadgets and using energy-saving light bulbs.

GLOSSARY

aquifer A layer of underground rock that contains water.

architecture The style and design of buildings.

arid Describing somewhere that does not receive enough rain for plants to grow.

barren Describing somewhere where nothing can grow.

caravan A group of traders travelling long distances together.

climate The ususal weather conditions in a particular area.

commune A settlement where people live close together and share some possessions and amenities.

depression A large dip in the ground.

desertification The process by which farmland becomes desert.

drought A period of unexpectedly low rainfall, which causes severe water shortages.

ecosystem All the plants and animals in a particular environment.

endangered At risk of becoming extinct.

erg A large area of shifting sand dunes in a desert.

extinction The process by which a species of plant or animal dies out completely.

four-wheel drive A car where power goes to all four wheels to help it to grip the surface of the road better.

global warming The gradual increase in temperatures around the world over a period of time.

indigenous Native to an area.

indigo A tropical plant that is used to create dark blue dye.

Islamic Relating to the religion Islam, which is practised by Muslims.

leeward Towards the sheltered side (downwind).

livestock Farm animals that are raised for meat or trade.

massif A compact group of mountains.

memorial Something that is put up so people will remember a person, thing or event.

migrants People who move to another country to live.

nomadic Describing people who move around rather than living in one place.

plateau A large area of high, level ground.

reptile A cold-blooded animal that lays eggs.

sandstone A type of red or brown rock made of sand or quartz.

savanna A large grassy area where only a few trees grow.

scholar Someone who studies a particular subject.

soil erosion The process by which the top layer of soil is washed away by water or blown away by the wind.

tarpaulin Heavy-duty waterproof cloth.

INDEX & FURTHER INFORMATION

Books

Deserts (Amazing Habitats) by Leon Gray (Franklin Watts, 2014)
Deserts (Geographywise) by Leon Gray (Wayland, 2014)
The Sahara Desert (Deserts Around the World) by Molly Aloian (Crabtree Publishing, 2012)

Websites

http://www.livescience.com/23140-sahara-desert.html
http://www.sciencekids.co.nz/sciencefacts/earth/desert.html

Engineers
Build
Models

Reagan Miller

Crabtree Publishing Company

www.crabtreebooks.com

Author
Reagan Miller

Publishing plan research and development:
Reagan Miller

Editor
Crystal Sikkens

Proofreader
Shannon Welbourn

Design
Samara Parent

Photo research
Reagan Miller
Crystal Sikkens

**Production coordinator
and prepress technician**
Samara Parent

Print coordinator
Margaret Amy Salter

Photographs
© Roger Ressmeyer/CORBIS: page 19
Dreamstime: cover (right)
iStockphoto: page 11 (left inset)
Shutterstock: oconnelll: page 18
Thinkstock: page 14 (left)
All other images by Shutterstock

Library and Archives Canada Cataloguing in Publication

Miller, Reagan, author
      Engineers build models / Reagan Miller.

(Engineering close-up)
Includes index.
Issued in print and electronic formats.
ISBN 978-0-7787-0093-7 (bound).--ISBN 978-0-7787-0100-2 (pbk.).--
ISBN 978-1-4271-9404-6 (pdf).--ISBN 978-1-4271-9400-8 (html)

      1. Models and modelmaking--Juvenile literature. 2. Engineers--
Juvenile literature. I. Title.

TA154.M55 2013   j688.1   C2013-906286-6
                                                C2013-906287-4

Library of Congress Cataloging-in-Publication Data

Miller, Reagan, author.
   Engineers build models / Reagan Miller.
       pages cm. -- (Engineering close-up)
       Includes index.
   ISBN 978-0-7787-0093-7 (reinforced library binding : alk. paper) -- ISBN 978-
0-7787-0100-2 (pbk. : alk. paper) --ISBN 978-1-4271-9404-6 (electronic pdf) --
ISBN 978-1-4271-9400-8 (electronic html)
   1. Engineering models--Juvenile literature. 2. Models and modelmaking--
Juvenile literature. 3. Engineering--Juvenile literature. I. Title.
   TA177.M55 2014
   620.001'1--dc23
                                        2013050336

Crabtree Publishing Company

www.crabtreebooks.com   1-800-387-7650

Printed in Canada/032014/MA20140124

Published in Canada
Crabtree Publishing
616 Welland Ave.
St. Catharines, Ontario
L2M 5V6

Published in the United States
Crabtree Publishing
PMB 59051
350 Fifth Avenue, 59th Floor
New York, New York 10118

Published in the United Kingdom
Crabtree Publishing
Maritime House
Basin Road North, Hove
BN41 1WR

Published in Australia
Crabtree Publishing
3 Charles Street
Coburg North
VIC 3058

Contents

Who designs our world?

Have you ever looked up at a **skyscraper** or down at your running shoes and wondered how these things were made? They were first created by **engineers**! Engineers are the people who **design** many of the things in our world. To design means to make a plan to do or build something that solves a problem.

skyscraper

running shoes

4

Engineers design technologies

The things engineers design are called **technologies**. A technology is anything people make that solves a problem or meets a need. For example, a car is a technology that meets people's need to get from place to place quickly.

Technology is all around us! An umbrella is a technology because it solves the problem of getting wet when it is raining outside.

Technologies take time

Engineers have important jobs. They use math, science, and **creative thinking** to design technologies. Long before people use a technology, such as a bridge, engineers have spent a lot of time designing it to make sure it works well and is safe.

Engineers spent more than 65 years designing the Golden Gate bridge in San Francisco, California, before building began!

Working together

Engineers often work together in groups to design technologies. Working in groups lets engineers share different ideas. Engineers **communicate** their ideas to the people they work with and other people outside of the group. To communicate means to write, speak, or draw to share information.

What do you think?

What are some ways you can communicate your ideas to people?

What is a model?

One way engineers communicate their ideas to others is by making **models**. A model is a **representation** of a real object. A model can show how different parts of an object work together. A model can also show how something looks.

This boy has made a model of an airplane. The model helps him learn how the parts of an airplane work together.

Map models

This map is a model of a garden. It gives us information about where different fruits and vegetables are planted. The map is a model because it helps us understand more about how the real garden looks.

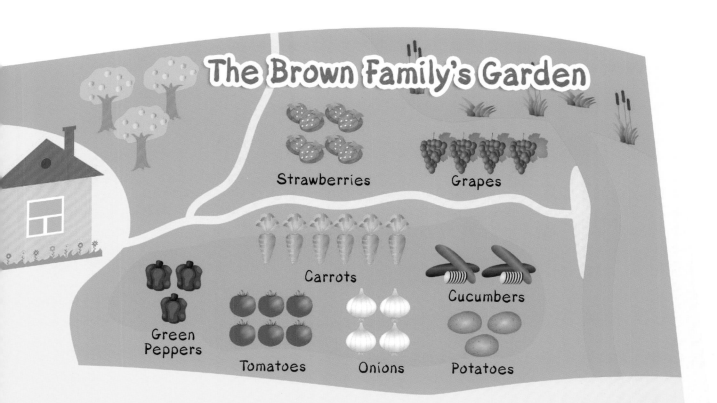

The Brown Family's Garden

Strawberries

Grapes

Carrots

Green Peppers

Tomatoes

Onions

Cucumbers

Potatoes

Alike but different

Models are not exactly like the things they represent. For example, some models may not have all of the same parts or **features** as the real thing. A toy car is a model of a real car. It has four tires and can move forward and backward, but it is much smaller and cannot move as fast as a real car.

Could you get a ride to school in a toy car?

Different parts

Models can be used to show things that are very large and have many different parts, such as a **wind turbine**. Building a real wind turbine would take a lot of time and cost a lot of money. A model turbine takes less time to build and shows how the different parts fit and work together.

blades

blades

The **blades** on this boy's model of a wind turbine spin like the blades on a real turbine.

11

Diagrams and blueprints

Some models are drawn on paper or made using a computer. A **diagram** is a drawing that shows the parts of an object and how it works. A diagram has labels. Labels are words that name or describe the different parts and help others understand the model better.

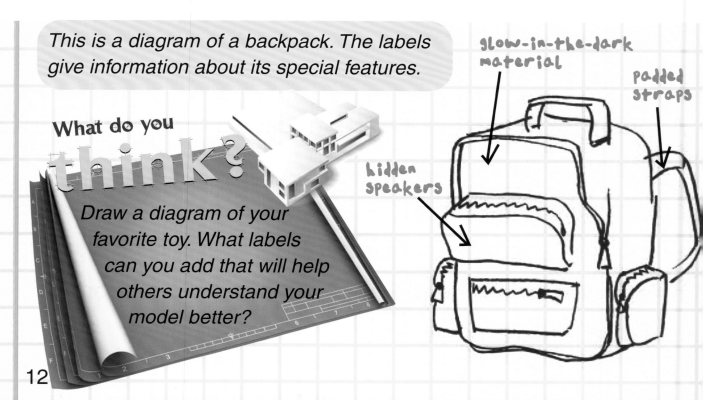

This is a diagram of a backpack. The labels give information about its special features.

glow-in-the-dark material

padded straps

hidden speakers

What do you think?

Draw a diagram of your favorite toy. What labels can you add that will help others understand your model better?

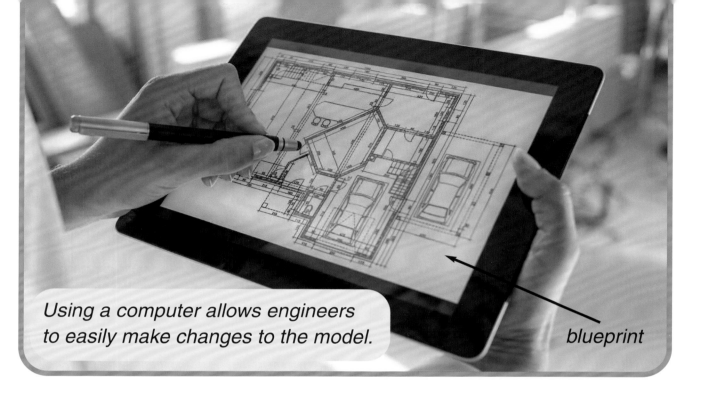

Using a computer allows engineers to easily make changes to the model.

blueprint

Blueprints

A **blueprint** is another kind of model that engineers use to show their design ideas to others. Blueprints are drawings that show the different parts of a building. For example, a blueprint for a school shows where the classrooms will be built. Engineers can draw blueprints on paper or using a computer.

Different forms

Models have different forms. For example, a map of the world and a globe are both models of Earth. Maps are flat, or **two-dimensional** models. They show length and width. A globe is a solid object. It is **three-dimensional.**

map

globe

3-D models

Three-dimensional models have length, width, and height. You can hold a three-dimensional model and look at it from above, below, and all sides. These kinds of models are also called 3-D models.

What do you think?

Give one example of another two-dimensional model and another three-dimensional model.

*A **diorama** is a kind of 3-D model. This diorama is a model of a house.*

15

How models are helpful

Models are helpful in many ways. Engineers make models to explain, or help people understand, their ideas for solving problems. People can review the model and give **feedback**, or suggestions, to the engineer to help make the design idea better.

This engineer is using a model to explain his idea to his team.

A designer, not a builder

Engineers do not make or build the things they design. The engineer can use their model to explain to the people who are building it how to build it properly. Engineers may visit the site where it is being built to make sure it is done correctly and answer any questions.

An engineer may design a bridge, but the engineer does not build the bridge.

Testing, testing

Engineers also build models to test their design ideas. Testing models helps engineers know if their ideas will work and are safe. They can also find out what changes they need to make to the model to make it better.

These students have made model cars. They are testing them to see which one will run the farthest using power from the Sun.

Shake tables move the same way as an earthquake. This allows the engineer to see the damage a home would receive in an earthquake.

shake table

Earthquake!

Earthquakes cause the ground to shake. They happen in many areas of the world. Engineers try to design houses that will receive the least amount of damage from shaking. Models of houses are tested on special tables called shake tables to see which designs work the best.

Engineers plan

Before making a model, engineers first make a plan. A good plan is important because it helps the engineer figure out how to make their model. **Materials** are an important part when planning a model. Materials are what objects are made of. Different materials have different **properties**. Properties describe how something looks, feels, or acts.

An engineer's plan includes:

☐ A sketch showing how they want the model to look

☐ A list of materials they will need to make the model

☐ The steps they will follow to make the model

Materials matter!

Choosing the best materials is an important part of building models. Some materials are better than others for making certain things. Would you wear rain boots made of cardboard? Of course not! Cardboard would let in water and make your feet wet. Rubber is a better material. Rubber is waterproof. It does not let water pass through.

A kite is made to fly in the air. To design a kite, an engineer would choose a material that is light so the kite can stay up in the air.

MY PLAN

Materials needed:
- scissors
- tape
- pieces of scrap paper
- string
- craft sticks

Steps to follow:
1. Cut paper into kite shape.

2. Tape craft sticks in the shape of a "t" on the back of the kite.

3. Tape string to the bottom of the kite.

Flying high!

In 1903, the Wright brothers made history when they became the first people to fly in an airplane. They spent more than four years building and testing thousands of different models.

Build your own model airplane using scrap paper. Try using different kinds of paper or change the shape of its wings. Which design flew the farthest?

Learning more

Books

The Three Little Pigs: An Architectural Tale. by Steven Guarnaccia.
Abrams Books for Young Readers, 2010.

Build It! Invent New Structures and Contraptions (Fact Finders)
by Tammy Enz. Capstone Press, 2012.

Websites

This website offers creative engineering challenges and the latest
engineering news for kids.
www.inventivekids.com

This website features interactive labs that explore forces, motion,
and shapes.
Building Big: The Labs:
pbs.org/wgbh/buildingbig/lab/index.html

Words to know

Note: Some bolded words are defined in the text

blades (bleyds) noun The turning part on a wind turbine. A blade looks like an airplane propeller.

creative thinking (KREE-ey-tiv thing-king) noun Being able to use your mind to create new and original ideas

features (FEE-cher) noun   A part or detail of something that stands out

representation (rep-ri-zen-TA-shuhn) noun Something that stands in place of another thing with similar features

skyscraper (SKAHY-skrey-per) noun A very tall building

wind turbine (wind TUR-bin) noun A windmill that changes wind energy into electricity

A noun is a person, place, or thing.

Index